Baptism

A Doctrinal Introduction

Cory Edward Kay Smith

WESTBOW
P R E S S®
A DIVISION OF THOMAS NELSON
& ZONDERVAN

WestBow Press books may be ordered through booksellers or by contacting:

WestBow Press
A Division of Thomas Nelson & Zondervan
1663 Liberty Drive
Bloomington, IN 47403
www.westbowpress.com
1 (866) 928-1240

ISBN: 978-1-9736-8537-1 (sc)
ISBN: 978-1-9736-8536-4 (e)

Print information available on the last page.

WestBow Press rev. date: 2/5/2020

This book is dedicated to my loving wife Kristy, who took the courage to present the gospel to me many years ago.

This book is dedicated to my parents and grandparents, who instilled in me the hard work and dedication that was needed to finish this work.

This book is dedicated to John MacArthur, a man I have never had the privilege of meeting, but who has helped and educated me in the Scriptures over the years more times than I can count.

This book is dedicated to my son Peyton, who will and always will be my greatest achievement.

This book is dedicated to my Grandad Frank, a man who holds a different interpretation to baptism than myself, but a man I will always love and respect for eternity.

Contents

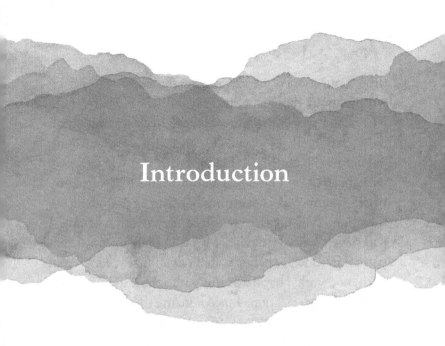

Introduction

Research and experience have shown that most readers skip the introduction of books and immediately start reading the first chapter. With that in mind, the introduction to this book will be very brief and to the point. The reason I chose to write this book was rather straightforward. After having put my trust in Christ for salvation, I was baptized shortly after. A few years later, however, my understanding of Christian baptism was challenged. I will be the first to admit that up until that point I had shown little concern for "rightly handling the word of truth" (2 Tim. 2:15). I downplayed the importance of "always being prepared to make a defense" for the correct interpretation of Scripture (1 Pet. 3:15). A conversation took place between me and a close relative, and after that conversation was held, I felt completely overwhelmed. I instantly started to doubt the doctrine I was taught to believe, and for the first time, I questioned my salvation experience. Had I been wrong about the gospel message all these years? Had I been led to believe a lie? To me, this was no small issue. After all, God chose men to be saved through "belief in the truth" (2 Thess. 2:13). But what exactly was the truth? The conversation that challenged my belief system was concerning baptism's relationship to salvation. Was baptism required for salvation or not? I had never really struggled with this issue up until that point. I had always believed that salvation was a matter of faith, not works; baptism falling into the latter category. However, the questions I faced during that conversation got me thinking. If the doctrine I believed was accurate, then why did my argument seem so uncompelling? I trusted in the deepest part about me that my salvation experience was genuine, but I still felt my understanding of Christian baptism was flawed. Time quickly passed as I struggled to build my understanding. After feeling led to enroll in seminary, I quickly determined that others who were being trained to pastorally lead churches had similar questions and experienced similar problems with this topic. Those men who were being trained to pastor churches still had unanswered questions about baptism. In my opinion, that was unacceptable, and it was precisely at that juncture where I decided to publish a book that endeavored to unfold a proper understanding on the subject. As a disclosure, I fully understand that I am not a biblical scholar by definition of the term. However, I have come to realize the countless importance of "examining the Scriptures daily" and "rightly handling the word of truth" (Acts 17:11; 2 Tim. 2:15). Without reservation,

I feel this book represents an accurate interpretation of the biblical material. Hopefully, it will provide some clarity to those searching for a deeper understanding on baptism.

John's Baptism

John the Baptist was more than a prophet (cf. Matt. 11:9). As the forerunner to the Messiah, John would fulfill the words spoken by the prophet Isaiah; "I am the voice of one crying out in the wilderness, 'Make straight the way of the Lord'" (John 1:23; cf. Isa. 40:3). After four hundred years of prophetic silence, that silence would finally be broken. His ministry began at a crucial point in history, and was unlike any other ministry that preceded it or that would follow. In one sense, John's life had a parallel to Old Testament prophets (cf. 2 Kings 1:8; Matt. 14:3; Mark 1:6). Yet, in other ways, aspects of his ministry were entirely unique. In Scripture, John is notoriously labeled as the *baptistēs* or literally the Baptizer (cf. Matt. 3:1; 11:11-12; 14:2, 8; 16:14; 17:13; Mark 6:14, 24-25; 8:28; Luke 7:20, 33; 9:19). As most are well aware, this label would distinguish John's vocation in ministry. But what actually spurred John to commence baptizing when he began his public ministry? This is a question that has often stumped many students of Scripture. It is also a question that has yielded many possible answers. For example, some have argued that John's baptism was an alteration of Jewish proselyte baptism. Those in favor of this view contend that John merely altered a Jewish rite that already existed at the time he began his ministry. At initial glance, this explanation seems rational. In fact, many respectable Bible teachers have upheld this view. For instance, Augustus Strong suggests, "It is probable that the baptism of John was an application to Jews of an immersion which, before that time, was administered to proselytes among the Gentiles."[1] John MacArthur has also upheld this view. He explains, "The Jews performed a similar one-time washing of Gentile proselytes, symbolizing their embrace of the true faith [of Judaism]."[2] Rabbinical literature does suggest there were, in effect, three requirements a Gentile had to undergo in order to be engrafted into Judaism. This ordinance required Gentiles to undergo the rite of circumcision, submit to a *tebilah*, and then offer a blood sacrifice. According to tradition, the *tebilah* (proselyte baptism) was a one-time immersion in water reserved for Gentiles. This act signified spiritual cleansing and visibly marked that person's joining to the community of Israel. Obviously, there is a strong attraction and convenience to

---

[1] Strong, Augustus. *Systematic Theology: A Compendium and Commonplace-Book Designed for the Use of Theological Students.* Wentworth Press, 2011. (Kindle Location 43708). Kindle Edition.
[2] MacArthur, John. *ESV MacArthur Study Bible* Good News Publishers/Crossway Books, 2010. (Kindle Location 106331). Kindle Edition.

suggest that proselyte baptism preceded John's baptism, and by doing so suggest that John's baptism was a replica of the *tebilah*. Unfortunately, however, the actual date for the origin of proselyte baptism cannot be strictly determined. As Everett Ferguson observes, "no mention of it occurs in Philo, Josephus, or Joseph and Aseneth." Ferguson further states, "The earliest literary account of the rabbinic conversion ceremony in the Babylonian Talmud is probably a *beraita*, that is, a source of Palestinian origin, probably from the second century. The practice may have been earlier, but how early is an assumption and so far lacking in definite proof."[3] Augustus Strong, despite his view on the matter, even notes, "Proselyte baptism is not mentioned in the *Mishna* (A.D. 200). The first distinct account of it is in the Babylonian Talmud (*Gemara*) written in the fifth century."[4] Although Ferguson and Strong disagree on the first appearance of proselyte baptism in historical literature, one thing is for certain; proselyte baptism apparently does not appear in historical literature prior to the second century. Consequently, no one can assertively claim that John's baptism was an imitation of proselyte baptism. The historical evidence simply does not support it. More importantly, the evidence to prove otherwise is nowhere found in Scripture. There is simply no instruction recorded in the Old Testament

---

[3] Ferguson, Everett. *Baptism in the Early Church: History, Theology, and Liturgy in the First Five Centuries.* Wm. B. Eerdmans Publishing Company, 2009. (Kindle locations 1995-2015). Kindle Edition.

[4] Strong, Augustus. *Systematic Theology: A Compendium and Commonplace-Book Designed for the Use of Theological Students.* Wentworth Press, 2011. (Kindle Location 43684). Kindle Edition.

that required a proselyte to receive baptism in order to be accepted as part of the Israelite community. The only requirement that Scripture affords is circumcision, assuming the proselyte was a male (cf. Exod. 12:48-49). During his earthly ministry, Jesus plainly taught that rabbinical tradition should not be equated to the "commandment of God" (cf. Mark 7:9). Consequently, I find it difficult to recommend that John merely imitated a rite that stemmed from rabbinical tradition. In fact, when John first began his ministry, the religious leaders sent others from Jerusalem to actually question his practice. They asked, "Why are you baptizing, if you are neither the Christ, nor Elijah, nor the Prophet?" (John 1:25). In their conversation they indicated that John's baptism, either in its form or application, was a new order that required special authority. This conversation held between the leaders of Israel and John suggests that John did not modify any existing rite but, quite the opposite, developed the rite himself. In fewer words, there was no specific instruction in the Law or Prophets that would persuade John to administer his baptism. If proselyte baptism did exist prior to John's baptism and John's baptism was an imitation thereof, that assumption lacks definite proof.

Even though historical evidence cannot prove proselyte baptism preceded John's baptism, many still argue that proselyte baptism must have existed before John's baptism and Christian baptism, for Jews would not have later copied a Christian rite. This position obviously has warrant, but such notions are hypothetical. In fact, there appears to be more similarities between proselyte baptism and Jewish purification rites than between proselyte baptism and John's baptism. Everett Ferguson actually lists these distinctions. As he points out, "Proselyte baptism required witnesses but was self-administered; baptism by John [and Christians] had an administrator." He also explains, "Proselyte baptism was [reserved] for Gentiles."[5] John's baptism, however, was largely reserved for Jewish people (cf. Matt.3:5; Mark 1:5). These differences make it difficult to see a clear relationship between the origin of John's baptism and proselyte baptism. Once again, neither scriptural proof nor historical evidence seems to support a correlation.

To explain the origin of John's baptism, many have suggested his baptism was related to the Old Testament rites of purification. This, too, is a practical assumption since the Mosaic Law did prescribe ceremonial applications of water for the purpose of purification. In the natural order of things, water serves as a cleansing agent. Therefore, it reasonably offered a means of restoration. Notably, the practice of purification both applied to persons and to inanimate objects. The term that applied to a defiled person or object was "uncleanness," and this label was attached to the person or object for various reasons (cf. Lev. 15:31). For example, if an individual came into contact with an unclean animal carcass, he was required to "wash his clothes and be unclean until evening" (Lev. 11:28). If an object was contacted, however, it was to be dipped rather than washed; it "must

---

[5] Ferguson, Everett. *Baptism in the Early Church: History, Theology, and Liturgy in the First Five Centuries.* Wm. B. Eerdmans Publishing Company, 2009. (Kindle location 2083). Kindle Edition.

be put into water" [εἰς ὕδωρ βαφήσεται] and would be unclean until evening (Lev. 11:32). Encountering certain disease would also require the person to undergo a similar treatment. For example, on the day the priest pronounced a leprous person's cleansing, he was required to "wash his clothes" and "bathe himself in water" (Lev. 14:8). Seven days following, he was once again required to wash his clothes and "bathe his body in water" in order to be truly reckoned clean (Lev. 14:9). The same rule would also apply to those who came into contact with a person who had a bodily discharge (see Leviticus 15). The assumption still stands that when a person was required to bathe his body, he was to be completely immersed (cf. Lev. 15:16). Allen Ross makes a very practical observation on this matter. He suggests, "The water was 'living water' taken from a spring and not from standing water. Fresh running water may have signified the new and fresh start of the [defiled] person" (see Lev. 14:5; 50-53; 15:13).[6] With all that being said, the significance behind these washings is not a complicated matter. God, in his grace, made provision for those who had become temporarily defiled to be restored to the covenant community. Therefore, the person who took that provision lightly and disobeyed the Law would "bear his iniquity" (Lev. 17:16). But the question still remains, "Is there a correlation between the Jewish rites of purification and John's baptism?" Many seem to agree that there is. In John's gospel, we observe that "a discussion arose between some of John's disciples and a Jew over purification" (John 3:25). Evidently, this

---

[6] Ross, Allen. *Holiness to the Lord*. Grand Rapids: Baker Publishing Group, 2006. (p. 289).

conversation was related to John's baptism. The word used for purification in this text is *katharismos*. Notably, this word is used only one other time in John's gospel, and there it specifically refers to the "Jewish rites of purification" (John 2:6). Whether or not that refers to Old Testament rites or to those developed under rabbinical tradition, one cannot be entirely sure.[7] Regardless, it appears that some of John's constituents did see a relationship between his baptism and the Old Testament rites of purification. One comparison, for example, can be seen in the manner by which John administered his baptism. As previously mentioned, most Old Testament cleansings required the person to bathe his "whole body in water" (cf. Lev. 15:16). In comparison, John's baptism also required the person to be fully immersed. When those from Jerusalem and Judea came to John, they were "baptized by him in the river Jordan" (Matt. 3:6; cf. Mark 1:5; Luke 3:3). In John 3:23, we also read that John was baptizing "at Aenon near Salim, because water was plentiful there." Simply stated, there would be little need to subject one's ministry around an abundant supply of water if immersion was not the manner by which John's baptism was administered.[8] Another piece of supporting evidence found in the

---

[7] In light of other scriptural passages, the latter is most likely true (cf. Matt. 7:3-5). Since almost all of the other New Testament occurrences of *katharismos* refer to the ceremonial laws of the Old Testament it is hard not to see that intention here (see Mark 1:44; Luke 2:22; 5:14; the exception being 2 Peter 1:9 where it is still translated purification).

[8] This interpretation only gains further support from the usage of *baptizo* in the LXX with reference to the act of immersion (see 2 Kings 5:14 for a specific example).

Gospels is the event of Jesus' baptism. When Jesus was baptized, he "immediately he went up from the water" (Matt. 3:16; cf. Mark 1:10). The passage strongly suggests that Jesus went down into the water during his baptism and came out from underneath it. Evidently John's baptism and the Old Testament laws *both* required the person to be fully immersed. This comparison, however, still doesn't provide sufficient evidence to assert the origin of John's baptism stemmed from Old Testament ceremonial cleansings. The differences between the two should also be noted. First, the purification rituals of the Old Testament were generally self-administered and were to be repeated if the impurity persisted. For example, if a man had a discharge that was considered regular, he was still required to bathe when he encountered his emission (cf. Lev. 15:3). In contrast, John's baptism was not self-administered and from what evidence Scripture affords, his baptism was not a reoccurring event for the individual. It was John who initially baptized "with water for repentance (μετανοία)" (Matt. 3:11). And although it is beyond the scope of this chapter, the biblical definition of μετανοία does not primarily refer to a moral change from sinful behavior towards righteous conduct, but to a change in one's relationship with God. So in that sense, John's baptism was unique because it was not to be repeated.

So, if John's baptism was not an imitation of either proselyte baptism or the Old Testament rites of purification, then where did it originate from? Or, if these prior explanations are not conclusive, then what is? We can rest assured that Scripture does afford a reasonable explanation. When Jesus confronted the chief priests, he questioned them concerning John's baptism: "The baptism of John, from where did it come? From heaven or from man?" (Matt. 21:25; cf. Mark 11:30; Luke 20:4). The question was evidently rhetorical. In this passage, Jesus explains that John's commission to baptize came directly from God. Therefore, it is probably a better interpretation of Scripture to conclude that John began baptizing after being led by God to do so. John's account seems to affirm this. "I myself did not know him, but for this purpose I came baptizing with water, that he might be revealed to Israel. I myself did not know him, but *he who sent me to baptize* with water said to me, 'He on whom you see the Spirit descend and remain, this is he who baptizes with the Holy Spirit'" (John 1:31, 33; *emphasis added*). So at the right time, according to God's instruction, "John appeared, baptizing in the wilderness and proclaiming a baptism of repentance for the forgiveness of sins" (Mark 1:4). In fewer words, the origin of John's baptism was a direct result of God's prompting. It was, at that time, unique to his ministry and unique to anything prescribed by the Mosaic Law.

After determining the source of John's baptism, one must also determine the candidates for receiving it. It's apparent from Scripture that John administered his baptism largely to the Jewish community.[9] There is no evidence in Scripture to support the contrary. As Paul

---

[9] See John 1:31; the purpose of John's baptism was to reveal Christ to Israel. See also Matt. 10:6 and Matt. 15:24 in reference to the earthly ministry of Jesus. Obviously, Christ did minister to Gentiles but he was predominately focused, at that time, on the

wrote in his letter to the Romans, "They are Israelites, and to them belong the adoption, the glory, the covenants, the giving of the law, the worship, and the promises. To them belong the patriarchs, and from their race, according to the flesh, is the Christ, who is God over all, blessed forever. Amen" (Rom. 9:4-5). If the purpose of John's ministry was to prepare others for the arrival of the Christ and the inauguration of His kingdom, then we would expect John to prepare those for whom the Christ was initially promised.

Now the question that deserves the most attention refers to the implication of John's baptism. What significance did John's baptism have? It's apparent from Scripture that John's message was met with a large response. "Jerusalem and all Judea and all the region about the Jordan were going out to him, and they were baptized by him in the river Jordan, confessing their sins" (Matt. 3:5-6; cf. Mark 1:5).[10] The word used here for confess is *exomologeo* and it carries the meaning to acknowledge or by implication fully agree. But what were these Jewish crowds in agreement with? The answer is found in the content of John's preaching. At the time of John's ministry, it was commonplace for the Jews to presume they were exempt from God's eternal judgment because of their racial heritage. This was precisely the sort of presumption

---

Jews who considered themselves unworthy of the kingdom. The same could be said about John's ministry.

[10] The participle *exomologoumenoi* (translated her as *confessing*) can either be interpreted that the crowds who came to John were baptized "*as they confessed their sins*" or "*because they confessed their sins.*" I tent to argue for the latter interpretation.

John the Baptist thoroughly rebuked. John repeatedly warned, "And do not presume to say to yourselves, 'We have Abraham as our father', for I tell you, God is able from these stones to raise up children for Abraham'" (Matt. 3:9). John simply rejected the Jew's notion that they could inherit the Kingdom of God simply because of their race. Instead he preached that the members of Israel could find acceptance with the Messiah and a holy God if they would genuinely repent from their sin. As I mentioned earlier, repentance does not primarily refer to a change from evil to righteous conduct, but to a change in man's ongoing relationship to God. Subsequently, the baptism of John was a baptism of conversion. It publically marked the individual's turning from sin to God that he might henceforth live in obedience to Him.[11] As Tom Schreiner observes, "The reference to repentance and the forgiveness of sins make clear that John's baptism is to be understood not merely in terms of ritual purification and religious observance, but as essentially moral and ethical."[12] It should also be noted at the outset of our study that baptism is always related to conversion. This, however, stimulates yet another question. Did John's baptism symbolize conversion or did it actually affect it? Several thoughts have emerged. For example, Ernst Lohmeyer argued that baptism actually effected conversion. However, his argument is somewhat unique.

---

[11] Murray-Beasley, G.R. *Baptism in the New Testament*. Grand Rapids: William B. Eerdman's Publishing Company, 1962/1973. (p. 34).

[12] Schreiner, T., & Wright, Shawn. *Believer's Baptism*. B & H Publishing Group, 2006. (p. 31). Nook Edition.

He insisted that John preached not a baptismal repentance but a repentance baptism. In his understanding, repentance did not lead a man to baptism. Instead, he came to baptism in order to receive it (i.e. repentance). In fewer words, Lohmeyer understood John's baptism as not only effecting conversion, but actually producing repentance.[13] Much needs to be said about this interpretation. First, Scripture does not warrant this conclusion. Matthew records, "But when he saw many of the Pharisees and Sadducees coming to his baptism, he said to them, 'You brood of vipers! Who warned you to flee from the wrath to come? Bear fruit in keeping with repentance'" (Matt. 3:7-8; cf. Luke 3:7-8). The implication from that passage is clear. John expected those who were already repentant to receive his baptism. Why else would the crowds have confessed their sins at the time of their baptism, if they had not already acknowledged their sin and were willing to demonstrate that confession publically? G.R. Beasley-Murray upheld another view. He disagrees with Lohmeyer on this matter, but still argues that our gospel writers saw "in baptism a divine work, the fruit of which was conversion." He further argues, "baptism presumes the activity of God, who therein accepts the baptized man turning to Him and makes of the act the pledge of his forgiveness and seal of the baptized into the Kingdom."[14]

---

[13] Murray-Beasley, G.R. *Baptism in the New Testament*. Grand Rapids: William B. Eerdman's Publishing Company, 1962/1973. (p. 34).

[14] Murray-Beasley, G.R. *Baptism in the New Testament*. Grand Rapids: William B. Eerdman's Publishing Company, 1962/1973. (p. 36).

Murray's interpretation has warrant, but it creates a widely differing view concerning the doctrine of salvation. The question that should be raised here hardly ever gets mentioned. <u>Did God, beginning with John the Baptist, alter the way men appropriate salvation?</u> As I previously mentioned, baptism simply isn't found in the writings of the Old Testament. If God did not require men to receive baptism before John's baptism *(or before the installation of Christian baptism for that matter),* then how did men appropriate salvation during those eras of human history? Unfortunately, this issue has been vastly overlooked by those who support the doctrine of baptismal salvation. In the Old Testament, spiritual salvation isn't discussed primarily in terms of salvation, but rather in terms of belonging to God and his covenant people. Markedly, this essentially began with Abraham. From that point forward, God's covenant with Israel was incorporated at two levels, one racial and the other spiritual. In one sense, all those who descended from the physical lineage of Abraham, Isaac, and Jacob, were properly labeled as the people of God. In another sense, only the "remnant" within Israel was related to God spiritually. So the people of God, at that time, were a mixed community. Ethnically, they included both believing and unbelieving Jews, but spiritually there was the believing remnant that made up the true or spiritual Israel.[15] It's equally important to distinguish the difference between the memberships of these two groups. The members of spiritual Israel

---

[15] Ferguson, Sinclair and Lane, Anthony N.S. and Ware, Bruce. *Baptism: Three Views.* Downers Grove: Intervarsity Press, 2009. (p. 43). Kindle Edition.

were never made acceptable to God as a result of their obedience. "For by works of the law no human being will be justified in his sight" (Rom. 3:20). God never intended the law to be a means of salvation. Instead, it only revealed God's perfect standard and affirmed that living up to that standard was impossible to meet in man's own strength. In effect, the very purpose of the law was to show man his need of God's mercy and forgiveness. Any Jew who presumed he could earn God's acceptance through personal obedience was obligated to keep the entire law, without exception. "For all who rely on works of the law are under a curse; for it is written, 'Cursed be everyone who does not abide by all things written in the Book of the Law, and do them" (Gal. 3:10). Keeping the Law perfectly is obviously impossible, that is except for the man Christ Jesus. The believing Jew, however, had a different understanding of the Law. He found himself crushed under the weight of the Mosaic Law and his inability to keep it. Consequently, his only option was to turn and plead for God's grace and forgiveness. "But the tax collector, standing far off, would not even lift up his eyes to heaven, but beat his breast, saying, 'God be merciful to me, a sinner!'" Jesus said, "I tell you, this man went down to his house justified, rather than the other. For everyone who exalts himself will be humbled, but the one who humbles himself will be exalted" (Luke 18:13-14). This passage in Luke is a prime example of Old Testament salvation. Any Jew who was unwilling to humble themselves and acknowledge how utterly sinful they really were, did not receive God's mercy and forgiveness. "For not all who are descended from Israel belong to Israel" (Rom. 9:6). And this was, in the majority, Israel's dilemma. They "trusted in themselves that they were righteous" (Luke 18:9). They assumed their physical lineage and obedience to the Mosaic Law secured their acceptance with an infinitely holy God. Paul addressed this matter head on in his letter to the Romans; "Israel, who pursued a law that would lead to righteousness did not succeed in reaching that law. Why? Because they did not pursue it by faith, but as if it were based on works" (Rom. 9:31-32). And here lies the issue. Spiritual salvation is not contingent on man's works, but on God's sovereign grace working solely through man's faith.

> "For by grace you have been saved through faith, and this is not your own doing; it is the gift of God, not a result of works, so that no one may best. For we are his workmanship, created in Christ Jesus for good works, which God prepared beforehand, that we should walk in them" (Eph. 2:8-10).

> "Now to the one who works, his wages are not counted as a gift but as his due. 5 And to the one who does not work but believes in him who justifies the ungodly, his faith is counted as righteousness" (Rom. 4:4-5).

Sadly, anyone who confuses or mingles the concepts of faith and works has misinterpreted the entire message of the Bible. "But if it is by grace, it is no longer on the basis of works; otherwise grace would no longer be grace" (Rom. 11:6). MacArthur may have said it best; "Every false religion of the world – whether a heretical branch of Christianity, a highly developed pagan religion, or primitive is founded on some form of salvation by works to please God."[16] I could not agree more. Paul dedicated the entire fourth chapter of Romans to explaining how men throughout all of history are justified solely by faith. In so doing, he appeals to Genesis 15:6; "Abraham believed God, and it was counted to him as righteousness." In other words, Abraham simply trusted in God's available revelation, and as a result God declared him righteous. If baptism does affect salvation, then how does the following comparison made in Romans have any bearing application for the Christian? "But the words 'it was counted to him' were not written for his [Abraham's] sake alone, but for ours also. It will be counted to us who believe in him who raised from the dead Jesus our Lord who was delivered up for our trespasses and raised for our justification" (Rom. 4:23-25; cf. Gal. 3:1-9). To respond, there would be no relevance to Paul's argument if baptism is the time and place salvation is applied to the individual. To put it plainly, baptism was never intended to be a means of salvation, just as circumcision and obedience to the law were never intended to be a means of salvation. These are the elements which testify to salvation, not procure it. God has always justified those who would simply believe. The same was true before and after the cross.

So, if John's baptism did not result in salvation, then what relationship did it have to salvation? In other

---

[16] MacArthur, John. *Romans 1-8: The MacArthur New Testament Commentary: Macarthur New Testament Commentary Series.* Chicago: Moody Publishers, 1991. (Kind Location 4976). Kindle Edition.

words, why does it appear to be so inextricably linked to conversion? Evidently, John's baptism was associated with the act of turning from sin towards God. There is no denying that claim. In fact, both Mark and Luke refer to it as a "baptism of repentance for the forgiveness of sins" (Mark 1:4; Luke 3:3). This relationship needs to be explained. First, the Old Testament plainly demonstrates that the approach to God's forgiveness is through repentance.

> "Seek the Lord while he may be found; call upon him while he is near; let the wicked forsake his way, and the unrighteous man his thoughts; let him return to the Lord, that he may have compassion on him, and to our God, for he will abundantly pardon" (Isa. 55:6-7).

> "Therefore I will judge you, O house of Israel, every one according to his ways, declares the Lord God. Repent and turn from all your transgressions, lest iniquity be your ruin. 31 Cast away from you all the transgressions that you have committed, and make yourselves a new heart and a new spirit! Why will you die, O house of Israel (Ezek. 18:30-31).

> "If my people who are called by my name humble themselves, and pray and seek my face and turn from their wicked ways, then I will hear from heaven and will forgive their sin and heal their land" (2 Chron. 7:14).

"Say to them, As I live, declares the Lord
God, I have no pleasure in the death of the
wicked, but that the wicked turn from his
way and live; turn back, turn back from your
evil ways, for why will you die, O house of
Israel?" (Ezek. 33:11).

"When God saw what they did, how they
turned from their evil way, God relented to
the disaster that he had said he would do to
them, and he did not do it" (Jonah 3:10).

From a biblical perspective, repentance occurs when
one recognizes his true sinful condition and then turns
by faith to the one who alone can remedy his situation;
God. "For godly grief produces a repentance that leads to
salvation" (2 Cor. 7:10). So when God sovereignly affects
man's salvation, there is both the expression of repentance
and faith that results in man's forgiveness (cf. Acts 5:31;
11:17-18; 2 Tim. 2:25; Eph. 2:8-9). As I mentioned earlier,
this *ordo salutis* (i.e. order of salvation) applied to those
who lived before, during, and after John's ministry. John
the Baptist, therefore, did not establish a different method
of salvation (e.g. administering baptism) as some might
presume. Instead he simply reiterated the foundational
truth of Scripture that Israel had willfully denied (cf.
Luke 1:76-79). Men could receive forgiveness if they
would sincerely repent from their sin (cf. Matt. 3:8). The
visible evidence of such change was to be demonstrated
in receiving baptism and continuing obedience. Once
again, John's baptism did not produce forgiveness. His
baptism did not do anything spiritually, but it did serve

as an important public demonstration. John required the members of Israel to agree they were outside the spiritual remnant of God's people *despite* their physical lineage. By submitting to John's baptism, they would therefore agree that God's righteousness was available through repentance. As MacArthur observes, "When John the Baptist baptized in water for repentance of sin, the clear and obvious intent was a turning to righteousness. In receiving John's baptism, the sinner renounced his sin and through symbolic cleansing henceforth identified himself with the [coming] Messiah and His righteousness."[17] So for those few in number who were truly saved at the time of John's ministry, baptism visibly marked the renouncing of sin and turning towards God. In other words, John's baptism vividly testified to one's conversion, but in no way did it procure it.

There are certainly other passages throughout the Gospels which confirm John's baptism did not affect salvation. For example, at the baptism of Jesus, John at first refuses to allow Jesus to receive his baptism. "John would have prevented him saying, 'I need to be baptized by you, and do you come to me?'" (Matt. 3:14). This, in large, is an overlooked passage. Those who argue that John's baptism affected the forgiveness of sins do not respectfully take into account this dialogue. If John's baptism did affect salvation, then John's desire and demand for baptism would lead us to believe that he was

---

[17] MacArthur, John. *Romans 1-8: The MacArthur New Testament Commentary: Macarthur New Testament Commentary Series.* Chicago: Moody Publishers, 1991. (Kind Location 6779). Kindle Edition.

in need of salvation despite having already having entered into public ministry. Another example occurs later during the ministry of Christ. Jesus saw an opportunity to confirm his identity as the Messiah in connection with the ministry of John the Baptist. Jesus said, "I tell you, among those born of women none is greater than John" (Luke 7:28). Very few at that time would have argued with that statement (cf. Luke 1:15). "When John's messengers had gone, Jesus began to speak to the crowds concerning John: 'What did you go out into the wilderness to see? A reed shaken by the wind'" (Luke 7:24)? At that time, the general populace had traveled miles to see John because they evidently thought he was a fulfillment to Old Testament prophecy (cf. Matt. 14:5; Luke 20:6). If these crowds had fully accepted John, then those who received John's baptism had no reason not to accept Jesus as the Messiah. Jesus forces this issue. He questions, "What then did you go out to see? A man dressed in soft clothing? Behold, those who are dressed in splendid clothing and live in luxury are [found] in kings' courts" (Luke 7:25). What did he mean by that? Well, in those times a man who dressed in soft clothing was considered effeminate. Here, it also refers to men who flattered those in political authority for their own reward or acceptance. However, John did not fit either of those descriptions. In fact, John opposed the authorities to their face on account of their sin (cf. Luke 3:19; Mark 6:20). As Jesus points out, John possessed all the characteristics of a genuine prophet. Jesus once again raises the question; "What then did you go out to see? A prophet? Yes, I tell you, and more than a prophet. This is he of whom it is written, 'Behold, I send my messenger before your face, who will prepare your way before you.' I tell you, among those born of women none is greater than John" (Luke 7:26-28). Jesus elevated the importance of John and his religious authority, and he did so for a very specific reason. Multitudes of Jewish crowds had come to John, received his baptism, and accepted him as the forerunner of Christ. However, those same people, who once followed John, were now rejecting the claims Jesus made as Messiah. In so doing, the general populace had essentially altered the purpose of John's ministry. To not accept Jesus as the Christ would force someone to deny John as the forerunner of Messiah. Ironically, Luke records, "When all the people heard this, and the tax collectors too, they declared God just, having been baptized with the baptism of John, but the Pharisees and the lawyers rejected the purpose of God for themselves, not having been baptized by him" (Luke 7:29-30; cf. Matt. 11:7-20). Many want to use this verse to support baptismal salvation, but the context should support a rather different conclusion. The dividing line is ultimately drawn between the ungodly and those who merely profess to be godly in character. The Pharisees and the Lawyers did not submit to John's baptism because they didn't consider themselves as defiled, unworthy sinners. Those who received John's baptism, however, were willing to acknowledge that claim and demonstrate it publically. When these people declared God just, they were simply in agreement with Jesus regarding John's ministry. And it's precisely at this juncture where people, in general, fail to rightly divide the truth. There were lots of Jews who received John's baptism, but they would eventually reject Jesus Christ. In other words, most of the people who received John's baptism provided little to no evidence of true conversion. As Jesus pointed out, "There is another who bears witness about me [John], and I know that the testimony that he bears about me is true. He was the burning and shining lamp, and *you were willing to rejoice for a while in his light*" (John 5:32, 35; *emphasis added*). The antecedent you is not just a reference to the religious authorities, but evidently to the nation of Israel as a whole. In short, those who submitted to John's preaching, in the majority, only did so for a short period. These crowds, at large, fit the description of the rocky ground in the Parable of the Soils. They heard the word from John's preaching and they immediately received it with joy (cf. Mark 1:16). They were enthusiastic to experience something radical and different (i.e. baptism) from the standards of Judaism. But like many who affiliate themselves with the church today, they had no root in themselves. Because there was no spiritual life in them, they endured his truth only for a season. When Jesus presented difficult truth, when he demanded a life of forsaking all, and when he pronounced his claim as Messiah, the general populace ultimately rejected him. These same crowds who came out to John, three years later were the ones yelling, "Crucify him! Crucify him!" As John explained, "Whoever believes in the Son has eternal life; *whoever does not obey the Son shall not see life*, but the wrath of God remains on him" (John 3:36; *emphasis added*). As always, the evidence of conversion is seen through obedience. Scripture records that Jerusalem and all Judea came out to receive John's baptism. When Christ ascended to the Father, however, only one-hundred and twenty were gathered in the upper room leading up to the events on Pentecost. One simply cannot overlook the difference between the number of those who received John's baptism and those who persevered to follow Christ until the very end. To suggest John's baptism effected spiritual salvation would indicate that the general populace who received John's baptism was spiritually saved.[18] However, Scripture leads us to draw an opposite conclusion. Not only did the majority of Israel reject the true identity of Jesus, but his demands to forsake all and follow him were largely ignored (cf. John 1:11). In the words of Christ, "Many are called, but few are chosen" (Matt. 22:14).

Although John administered baptism, Scripture records that "Jesus himself did not baptize, but only his disciples" (John 4:2). In the context of the current passage, this is a parenthetical statement, which relates to the sentence: "Jesus was making and baptizing more disciples than John" (John 4:1; cf. John 3:22). In other words, Jesus did not personally baptize anyone. As I will mention in a later chapter, it also appears that this portion of his ministry was only temporary in nature. As MacArthur points out, "If baptism were a condition for salvation, He would have been baptizing people; after all, He came to seek and to save that which was lost (cf. Luke 19:10)."[19]

---

[18] If John's baptism did inaugurate a different means or method of appropriating salvation, then why did Jesus insist that salvation could still be found in the books of Moses and the Prophets during his public ministry knowing that baptism was unique Old Testament revelation (cf. Luke 16:16, 31)?

[19] MacArthur, John. *The Gospel According to Jesus*. Grand Rapids: Zondervan Publishing Group, 1988. (p. 63). Nook Edition.

Perhaps the most convincing evidence in the Gospels that lead us to believe baptism is not required for salvation are those passages which testify of salvation apart from baptism. The penitent woman, the publican, the paralytic man, and the thief on the cross all experienced salvation apart from baptism (see Luke 7:37-50; Luke 18:13-14; Matt. 9:2; Luke 23:39-42 respectively). For that matter, there is no specific record that the apostles were baptized, yet Jesus pronounced them clean through the "word" that he had spoken to them (John 15:3). "Truly, truly, I say to you, *whoever hears my word and believes him who sent me has eternal life.* He does not come into judgment, but has passed from death to life" (John 5:24; *emphasis added*). Luke also records a similar thought; "The ones along the path are those who have heard; then the devil comes and takes away the word from their hearts, *so that they may not believe and be saved"* (Luke 8:12; *emphasis added*). Both of these passages explain a clear truth represented by all of Scripture. "Faith comes by hearing and by hearing through the word of Christ" (Rom. 10:17). Once again, salvation is not affected by man's works but by God's grace through faith alone.

In conclusion, there are some other points that can be made about John's baptism. First, there is an eschatological significance to John's ministry and subsequently to his baptism. As Murray explains, "He [John] is himself an eschatological figure, whose activity sets in motion the process that shall [presumably] culminate in the judgment and the redemption of the Messiah."[20] John was

---

[20] Murray-Beasley, G.R. *Baptism in the New Testament.* Grand Rapids: William B. Eerdman's Publishing Company, 1962/1973.

trying to prepare Israel for the restoration of the kingdom. However, Israel rejected their King and subsequently the Kingdom of God. As a result, the establishment of the prophesied kingdom has been delayed (Ps. 10:16, 29:10, 145:13, Dan. 2:44, 4:3).[21] Secondly, the prevailing location of John's ministry may have further significance. John baptized in and near the Jordan River, which has led many commentators to suggest John's baptism signified a new Exodus for Israel. Dumbrell explains that John encouraged the nation to "go back to the beginning of its journey, back to the crossing of the Jordan, and once again set out into the Promised Land, but this time in a new national direction into a new eschatological age."[22] One can easily see the similarities, but the interpretation cannot be forced. I personally, however, tend to agree with Dumbrell's assessment. Thirdly, the ultimate purpose of John's baptism is best described from Scripture. The apostle John records, "There was a man sent from God, whose name was John [the Baptist]. He came as a witness, to bear witness about the light [Jesus Christ], that all might believe through him" (John 1:6-7). "For this purpose I [John] came baptizing with water, that he [Christ] might be revealed to Israel" (John 1:31) John did, in fact, bear faithful witness to Jesus Christ. However, God provided a greater witness through John's ministry when the Spirit of God descended on Christ at

(p. 32).

[21] See Alva J. McClain's book *The Greatness of the Kingdom* for a thorough study on the Kingdom of God.

[22] Cole, Graham. *He Who Gives Life*. Wheaton: Crossway Books, 2007 (p. 157).

his baptism. This would provide greater clarity that Jesus was the Messiah (cf. Luke 4:18). As would be expected of any faithful New Testament figure, John's baptismal ministry ultimately pointed to Jesus Christ. If all of God's promises find their fulfillment in Christ, then why would we expect the "greatest" prophet who ever lived to not illustrate that same basic truth (1 Cor. 1:20; Matt. 11:11; John 1:29-34). Subsequently, an obedient church will take into consideration the importance of John's preaching, the understanding of his baptism, and the example he set for others who would faithfully follow our Lord Jesus.

The Baptized Messiah

"Then Jesus came from Galilee to the Jordan to John, to be baptized by him" (Matt. 3:13; cf. Mark 1:9). This topic is more complex than often recognized. Many interpretations attempt to explain why Jesus was baptized, which has made this subject more difficult to understand than probably what it should be. I must admit, it is difficult to fully comprehend why Jesus came to receive John's baptism. Because so much has been said previously by other authors, I hesitate to share my own views on the subject. One thing is for certain, Jesus did have a specific reason for coming to receive John's baptism. As MacArthur notes, the aorist passive infinitive (*baptisthēnai*) suggests Jesus had a specific purpose for receiving baptism (Matt. 3:11).[23] So why exactly did Jesus

---

[23] MacArthur, John. *Matthew 1-7: The MacArthur New Testament Commentary.* Chicago: Moody Publishers, 1985. (p. 75). Kindle Edition.

come to receive John's baptism and what importance did he actually attach to his reception of it?

Scripture indicates that Jesus came from Nazareth of Galilee alone. Evidently no family members or friends accompanied him, and he had not yet officially called any disciples. He came, however, at a time "when all the people were [being] baptized" (Luke 3:21). So despite his solitary journey, his baptism would not be held in private or in secret fashion. It would be seen and openly witnessed by many of the general populace (cf. Acts 10:37-38). When Jesus came to receive John's baptism, however, he was not initially met with approval. "John would have prevented him, saying, 'I need to be baptized by you, and do you come to me?'" (Matt. 3:14). The Greek text implies that John's attempt to prevent Jesus was anything but subtle. He was sincerely, although insistently, trying to prevent Jesus from receiving his baptism. After all, John's baptism was a baptism associated with repentance. How could Jesus receive a baptism that represented the confession and forgiveness of sin? As Paul so plainly wrote, "For our sake he made him to be sin who knew no sin, so that in him we might become the righteousness of God" (2 Cor. 5:21; cf. Heb. 4:15; 9:14). This clearly seems to be the issue that prevents John, at first, from allowing Jesus to proceed. As MacArthur notes, "Among John's many God-given insights into whom Jesus was, what He was like, and what He had come to do, was his knowledge that the One who stood before Him was without sin."[24]

---

[24] MacArthur, John. *Matthew 1-7: The MacArthur New Testament Commentary.* Chicago: Moody Publishers, 1985. (p. 77). Kindle Edition.

Unfortunately, there will always be those who deny this claim. They have essentially argued from silence that Jesus received John's baptism because he, like the rest of humanity, was sinful. To make such a notion, however, opposes John's immediate concern. John resisted baptizing Jesus for the opposite reason that he resisted baptizing the religious leaders. They were in need of repentance, but they were unwilling to acknowledge their true spiritual condition. By contrast, Jesus came to receive John's baptism, though He alone had no need of repentance. "Which one of you convicts me of sin?" (John 8:46). "He who committed no sin, neither was deceit found in his mouth" (1 Pet. 2:22; cf. Isa. 53:9). Others have agreed that Jesus was morally perfect, but have wrongly suggested that he wasn't aware of his moral perfection or his long anticipated role as Messiah. They argue that Jesus did not receive endorsement of his Messianic role until those events that took place during his baptism. This position has not gained a lot of acceptance historically for several reasons. First, it would imply that Jesus came to receive John's baptism for the same reason the other Jews came to receive baptism. Secondly, Scripture leads us to defend the contrary. Jesus, even at a young age, appears to have an awareness of his Messianic role and task. When Joseph and Mary were searching for Jesus, he replied, "Why were you looking for me? Did you not know that I must be in my Father's house?" (Luke 2:49). There is simply no evidence from Scripture to recommend Jesus was not aware of his spiritual perfection at the time he received his baptism. If anything, his baptism only affirmed convictions already nurtured in his mind. As Murray contends, "When Jesus came to receive John's baptism, he must have went as one convinced of his vocation to be the Messiah and therefore as a representative person."[25] Still, others have taken his baptism as the occurrence where Jesus was bestowed with deity as a result of the Spirit's anointing. This explanation simply does not fit the context of the present passage, neither is it supported from the clear teaching of Scripture. In his humanity, Christ is always one, unconfused person in possession of two natures; one divine, one human (cf. Luke 2:11; John 1:1-18). In effect, the Incarnation was not a loss of divine attributes but an addition to human ones. "Though he was in the form of God, [he] did not count equality with God a thing to be grasped, but emptied himself, by taking the form of a servant, being born in the likeness of men" (Phi. 2:6-7). To put it plainly, the Son never stopped being God when he became a man (cf. Luke 1:32, 35). Jesus merely limited his expression of deity by accepting the limitations of a human nature.

So why did Jesus, who was even more aware of His own sinlessness than John, want to receive a baptism that testified to the renouncing of sin and turning towards God? His sole response; "Let it be so now, for thus it is fitting for us to fulfill all righteousness" (Matt. 3:15). Although the precise meaning of this verse is open for discussion, the general meaning is clear. Jesus understood John's reluctance and knew it was sincere. However, he gave permission for John to perform what he would have

---

[25] Murray-Beasley, G.R. *Baptism in the New Testament*. Grand Rapids: William B. Eerdman's Publishing Company, 1962/1973. (p. 56).

never been willing to do without proper instruction.[26] Clearly, this particular baptism was necessary to accomplish God's divine plan for both the ministries of John and Jesus. So, it must first be said that Jesus, who was fully aware of his Messianic role, came to receive baptism in response to the will of God.

Although baptism was not an ordinance required by the Mosaic Law, Jesus evidently saw John's baptism as an imposed obligation. And although his situation was unique from all others who received John's baptism, there is significance to this attitude expressed by Jesus. As MacArthur notes, "By submitting to John's baptism, it appears that Jesus acknowledged John's standard of righteousness was valid and in action affirmed it as the will of God to which men are to be subject."[27] Jesus thereby accredited John as the forerunner to his own public ministry. "For John came to you in the way of righteousness, and you did not believe him, but the tax collectors and the prostitutes believed him. And even when you saw it, you did not afterward change your minds and believe him" (Matt. 21:32).

The baptism of Jesus must also represent his willful identification with sinners. Kostenberger makes an important note in regard to this thought: "While the Messiah does not share with others baptized by John

---

[26] MacArthur, John. *Matthew 1-7: The MacArthur New Testament Commentary.* Chicago: Moody Publishers, 1985. (p. 77). Kindle Edition.

[27] MacArthur, John. *Matthew 1-7: The MacArthur New Testament Commentary.* Chicago: Moody Publishers, 1985. (p. 77). Kindle Edition.

the need for repentance and the forgiveness of sins, he voluntarily subjects himself to this rite as part of his identification with humanity and of his role as Savior of mankind."[28] After all, he came "in the likeness of sinful flesh," and would be "numbered with the transgressors" (Rom. 8:3; Isa. 53:12). When he received a baptism specifically reserved for sinners, it would mark his first public identification with those he came to save (cf. Luke 5:32; 19:10). As MacArthur rightfully adds, "He could not purchase righteousness for mankind if He did not identify with mankind's sin."[29]

As we have already determined, Jesus did not lose his divinity in becoming a man. He was still fully God in every way. In his deity he needed nothing. Yet, Jesus "had to be made like his brothers in every respect, so that he might become a merciful and faithful high priest in the service of God, to make propitiation for the sins of the people" (Heb. 2:17). In his humanity, Christ had to live an equivalent life to us, "yet without sin" in order for his sacrifice to be effective (cf. Heb. 4:15). In so doing, he would display an example of obedience for humanity to follow (cf. 1 Pet. 2:21; John 13:15; Phil. 2:5). Jesus would not only be submissive to the Father's will, but he would be dependent on the Holy Spirit (cf. Acts 10:38). In other words, he would not fulfill his Messianic responsibility relying on his own strength (*which was more than*

---

[28] Schreiner, T., & Wright, Shawn. *Believer's Baptism*. B & H Publishing Group, 2006. (p. 35). Nook Edition.

[29] MacArthur, John. *Matthew 1-7: The MacArthur New Testament Commentary.* Chicago: Moody Publishers, 1985. (p. 77). Kindle Edition.

sufficient to accomplish his task), but instead he would rely on the strength provided by the other two members of the Godhead. Markedly, this special anointing of the Spirit came at the time of his baptism; "And when Jesus was baptized, immediately he went up from the water, and behold, the heavens were opened to him, and he saw the Spirit of God descending like a dove and coming to rest on him" (Matt. 3:16). The Spirit's anointing, then, would enable the man Jesus to fulfill his earthly ministry that would eventually culminate at the cross (cf. Heb. 9:14). At his baptism, Jesus was therefore fully equipped to complete his humanly and Messianic task.

The Spirit's descending on Jesus would not only empower him for his earthly ministry, but it would also fulfill Old Testament prophecy. There were several Messianic prophecies that predicted the Spirit's anointing of the Messiah. "And the Spirit of the LORD shall rest upon him" (Isa. 11:2; cf. Isa. 42:1; 61:1). After his baptism, Jesus announced that he had indeed fulfilled this portion of Scripture (cf. Luke 4:17-21; Isa. 61:1-2a). John's baptism, then, played a crucial role in unveiling the true identity of Jesus Christ. John "came as a witness, to bear witness about the light, that all might believe through him" (John 1:7; cf. 1:31). But how would John's baptism accomplish this particular task? During his baptism, God's Spirit would visibly rest on Jesus and, therefore, satisfy the predictions of the Old Testament. "And John bore witness: 'I saw the Spirit descend from heaven like a dove, and it remained on him. I myself did not know him, but he who sent me to baptize with water said to me, 'He on whom you see the Spirit descend and remain, this is he who baptizes with the Holy Spirit.' And I have seen and have borne witness that this is the Son of God" (John 1:32-34). Markedly, the voice at Jesus' baptism also establishes a regal context; "This is my beloved Son" (Matt. 3:17). As Murray observes, "This is most naturally taken as an echo of Psalms 2:7, interpreted as a divine acclamation of the King-Messiah."[30] The Gospels reveal to us that Jesus holds all the qualities of God's appointed King. He offered the kingdom of God. He ruled over the elements of nature. He displayed his authority over demons and the spiritual world. The blind received their sight and even the lame were made to walk. It is not unexpected, then, to observe our Lord regarding this Kingdom as his very own (cf. Luke 22:30). Yet, this same King would also be God's anointed Servant (Matt. 3:17b; cf. Isa. 42:1). As Isaiah predicted, this Servant would suffer humiliation and persecution. "He was despised and rejected by men, a man of sorrows and acquainted with grief; and as one from whom men hide their faces he was despised, and we esteemed him not" (Isa. 53:3). At initial glance, this seems to be a paradox. How could God's appointed King endure such rejection? In response, the anticipated Messiah of Old Testament prophecy would not reach his rightful place of eminence by the usual means of political power or carnal force. On the contrary, he would be highly exalted through his own suffering and humiliation (cf. Phil. 2:7-11; Isa. 53:10-12). Through his life and ministry, Jesus proved himself to be the Servant of God who not only

---

[30] Murray-Beasley, G.R. *Baptism in the New Testament.* Grand Rapids: William B. Eerdman's Publishing Company, 1962/1973. (p. 50).

came to serve but to offer himself as the perfect sacrifice for sin. The voice heard at his baptism, then, appears to unite these two Messianic concepts of King *and* Servant that would depict our Lord's earthly ministry and affirm the necessity of the cross.

The baptism of Jesus also marked the beginning of his public ministry. As Murray notes, "Jesus came to the baptism of John among the penitents of Israel responsive to John's proclamation to begin the messianic task in its fullness."[31] Some have disagreed with this claim, but the Scriptural evidence is conclusive. Up until this point in the Gospels (i.e. the baptism of Jesus), we have only learned about the genealogy of Christ, the events which surrounded his birth, the exposition of John the Baptist, and an excerpt from Luke that provides a small insight to Jesus at a young age (Matt. 1-2, Luke 1-2). Shortly after His baptism, however, Scripture records that "Jesus began to preach, saying 'Repent, for the kingdom of heaven is at hand'" (Matt. 4:17; Mark 1:12-14; Luke 3:23). This passage, and others like it, strongly suggests that Jesus began his ministry following his baptism (cf. Acts 10:37-38; Acts 13:24). When Peter later assigned the selection process for Judas's successor, he required the candidates to have witnessed the Lord's entire earthly ministry "beginning with the baptism of John" (Acts 1:22).

Did the baptism of Jesus also prefigure his death? Most commentators seem to suggest it did. To support

---

[31] Murray-Beasley, G.R. *Baptism in the New Testament.* Grand Rapids: William B. Eerdman's Publishing Company, 1962/1973. (p. 55).

this conclusion, most have typically referred to the passages recorded in Mark and Luke.

> "Jesus said to them, 'You do not know what you are asking. Are you able to drink the cup that I drink, or to be baptized with the baptism with which I am baptized?'" (Mark 10:38).

> "I have a baptism to be baptized with, and how great is my distress until it is accomplished!" (Luke 12:50).

As Murray observes, "If those two passages read back into the baptism of Jesus, this truth was not explained." He further adds, "It is antecedently likely that the metaphor of baptism was taken from common usage. There is therefore some reason for assuming that the verb 'baptize' was capable of yielding a literal and figurative sense, without undue confusion."[32] I would agree that baptize can be, and often was, used figuratively (cf. 1 Cor. 10:2). However, is it merely coincidental that Jesus would use the word βάπτισμα when referring to his own death knowing baptism by immersion visibly pictures death and resurrection? Even though this argument is made from silence, it would seem that the widely accepted view (i.e. *the baptism of Jesus prefigured his death*) is to be retained until more convincing evidence to the contrary is advanced. If this conclusion is accurate, then the baptism of Jesus must

---

[32] Murray-Beasley, G.R. *Baptism in the New Testament.* Grand Rapids: William B. Eerdman's Publishing Company, 1962/1973. (p. 55).

have certainly foreshadowed the significance of Christian baptism (cf. Rom. 6:3; Col. 2:11-12). Unfortunately, no one establishes this correlation in the New Testament. So with that being said, there is no explicit evidence provided from Scripture to enforce this interpretation.

In summary, Jesus came to receive John's baptism in response to the sovereign will of God. Not only would Jesus accredit John as the forerunner of his own ministry, but by submitting to his baptism, Jesus would identify with sinful humanity. When Jesus received baptism, Old Testament prophecy was fulfilled. The Messiah was anointed with the Holy Spirit and affirmed by the Father's voice. Thus, the baptism of Jesus was the first public act recorded in Scripture that revealed to Israel his true identity as Messiah (cf. John 1:31-34). As a man, Christ would serve as our ultimate example. He would be wholly submissive to the Father's will and be entirely reliant on the Holy Spirit. After the Spirit's anointing, Jesus begins his Messianic task in its fullness, which marks the inception of his public ministry. From that point forward, it would be imperative that John decrease and the ministry of Christ increase. Jesus would set the ultimate example for believers, he would unfold God's truth in a way no man had ever seen, and most importantly, he would solely accomplish our redemption through the suffering of the cross.

The Baptism with the Holy Spirit

In the present chapter, my objective is to thoroughly explain what the baptism with the Holy Spirit is and how it relates to both the church and Christian baptism. At initial glance, it would appear that there are two primary views on this subject. Historically, one side of the debate interprets that Spirit baptism occurs at the time of conversion, while the other side believes this event occurs sometime after conversion. The former argues this is a common experience reserved for all Christians, whereas the latter contends the baptism with the Holy Spirit is limited to a select few within the church. To make matters even more complicated, there are a number of other positions that do exist. As is so often the case in a crucial doctrine, it has been exposed to truth and some error in terms of its interpretation. For example, some commentators have taught that being baptized with the Holy Spirit is "not a contrast of a Christian baptism in water and a Christian baptism in the Spirit; rather, the contrast is with John's water baptism without the Spirit."[33] In other words, some have taught that Spirit baptism actually occurs during water baptism. Wheeler Robinson apparently upheld this view. He explained, "Baptism, in its *New Testament* context, is always a baptism of the Spirit."[34] E.Y. Mullins, a Baptist theologian, upheld a similiar view. He understood the baptism of the Spirit as the baptism into the local church, implying that literal water baptism is a Spirit guided activity.[35] Dale Moody, another well-known theologian, taught that, "God imparts the Spirit in [water] baptism."[36] According to this position, there would be no distinction between the baptism with the Holy Spirit and the water baptism administered to believers. I will be the first to admit that these men have all made commendable arguments. However, I still believe their arguments are unsatisfactory to our biblical text. Consequently, we must attempt to obtain the general and appropriate teaching of Scripture on the subject of Spirit baptism.

At initial glance, there appears to only be seven passages in the New Testament where Spirit baptism is referenced. The first four are recorded in the Gospels:

---

[33] Ferguson, Everett. *Baptism in the Early Church: History, Theology, and Liturgy in the First Five Centuries*. Grand Rapids: William. B. Eerdmans Publishing Company, 2009. (p. 166). Kindle Edition

[34] *Baptist Principles*, 3rd ed. 1938, pp. 27, 77

[35] Mullins, E. Y. *International Standard Bible Encyclopedia*. Grand Rapids: William B. Eerdman's Publishing Company, 1943). (p. 399-401).

[36] Moody, Dale. *The Word of Truth*. Grand Rapids: Eerdmans, 1981). (p. 447).

Matthew 3:11: "I baptize you with water for repentance, but he who is coming after me is mightier than I, whose sandals I am not worthy to carry. He will baptize you with the Holy Spirit and fire."

Mark 1:8: "I have baptized you with water, but he will baptize you with the Holy Spirit."

Luke 3:16: "John answered them all, saying, 'I baptize you with water, but he who is mightier than I is coming, the strap of whose sandals I am not worthy to untie. He will baptize you with the Holy Spirit and fire."

John 1:33: "I myself did not know him, but he who sent me to baptize with water said to me, 'He on whom you see the Spirit descend and remain, this is he who baptizes with the Holy Spirit.'"

As Wayne Grudem notes, "It is hard to draw any conclusions from these four passages [alone] with respect to what baptism with the Holy Spirit really is."[37] However, there are some assumptions that can be made. First, John explains that this baptism will occur sometime in the future when compared to his own ministry. Secondly, John explains that Jesus would be the sole administrator of this baptism (cf. John 1:33). And lastly, the "baptism with the Holy Spirit" would contrast John's baptism. John

---

[37] Grudem, Wayne. *Systematic Theology: An Introduction to Biblical Doctrine.* Grand Rapids: Zondervan, 2009. (p. 766). Kindle Edition.

baptized with water, but according to John, Jesus would baptize with the agency or medium of the Holy Spirit.

Two additional passages are recorded in Acts that refer to the baptism with the Holy Spirit and are linked to the events of Pentecost:

> Acts 1:5: "for John baptized with water, but you will be baptized with the Holy Spirit not many days from now."[38]

> Acts 11:16-17: "And I remembered the word of the Lord, how he said, 'John baptized with water, but you will be baptized with the Holy Spirit.' If then God gave the same gift to them as he gave us when we believed in the Lord Jesus Christ, who was I that I could stand in God's way?"

These two passages reveal that whatever we may understand the baptism with the Holy Spirit to be, it certainly happened on the day of Pentecost when the Holy Spirit fell in great power on the disciples, and when the Holy Spirit fell on the Gentiles in Caesarea (cf. Acts 2:1-4; Acts 10:44-48).[39] It is equally important to distinguish that all six of the previous verses use almost exactly the same [grammatical] expression in Greek, with the only differences being some variation in word order or verb tense to fit the sentence, and with one example having the

---

[38] The ESV translators distinguish that ἐν could be translated in.

[39] Pentecost evidently marks the beginning of the church as a functioning body when the baptizing work with the Holy Spirit actually began.

preposition understood rather than expressed explicitly.[40] In fewer words, is it logical to agree that these passages relate to the same event.

The only remaining reference in the New Testament is in Paul's letter to the Corinthians:

> 1 Corinthians 12:13: "For in one Spirit we were all baptized into one body – Jews or Greeks, slaves or free – and all were made to drink of one Spirit." [41]

---

[40] Grudem, Wayne. *Systematic Theology: An Introduction to Biblical Doctrine.* Grand Rapids: Zondervan, 2009. (p. 766). Kindle Edition.

[41] It is no small debate whether to apply 1st Corinthians 12:13 to a baptism *with* the Holy Spirit, a baptism *by* the Holy Spirit, or water baptism. In response, the English translations that read "by one Spirit" cannot be supported by an examination of the Greek text. Paul writes *en heni pneumati...ebaptisthemen* ("in one Spirit ... we were baptized"). As Grudem points out, "Apart from one small difference (Paul refers to "one Spirit" rather than the "Holy Spirit"), all other elements are the same as the other verses that label a baptism *with* the Holy Spirit: the verb is *baptizo*, and the prepositional phrase contains the same words (*en* plus the dative noun *pneumati*)." If our translators are willing to translate baptize *in* or *with* the Holy Spirit in the other six New Testament occurrences, then it seems only proper to translate it the same way in its seventh occurrence (cf. Matt. 3:11; Mark 1:8; Luke 3:16; John 1:33; Acts 1:5; Acts 11:16). Many scholars have suggested that the reason various translators chose to use the word "by" as opposed to "with" or "in" in 1st Corinthians 12:13 is because the verse states that we are "baptized into one body." However, this implies a proper distinction. The Spirit is never suggested throughout Scripture to be the baptizer of an individual, but the medium or element of which a person is immersed. Christ is still

This last passage is essential to understanding this particular subject. As Paul explains, this is an event reserved for *all* Christians, without exception. With that being said, this baptism "in one Spirit" must occur at conversion. For one cannot belong to the body of Christ (i.e. the true church) without the indwelling of the Holy Spirit (cf. Rom. 8:9). Furthermore, this passage also concludes that the indwelling of the Spirit has a causal relationship to the baptism "in one Spirit". In other words, upon the indwelling of the Spirit, it's imperative to acknowledge that the "baptism with the Holy Spirit" has also occurred, or *vice versa* (cf. Acts 11:16-18). So in the mind of Paul, *all* believers not only become full members of Christ's body, but (inseparable from this occurrence) the Holy Spirit is also placed within each of them "in whom the whole structure, being joined together, grows into a holy

---

the implied baptizer. To ensure this is the correct interpretation, 1st Corinthians 10:2 should be observed. This text provides a parallel expression. In 1st Corinthians 10:2, the cloud and the sea are elements or mediums that overwhelmed the nation of Israel. The result of that particular "baptism" or immersion was solidarity into the spiritual leadership of Moses. The verse explains that the sea and the cloud were the elements into which the nation was immersed. The submission to the spiritual leadership of Moses was the location in which they found themselves after experiencing this particular immersion. This distinction can certainly be applied to 1st Corinthians 12:13; the Holy Spirit was the element in which the individual members of the church were baptized, and the body of Christ (i.e. the church) was the location in which they found themselves after experiencing this baptism. Therefore, it only seems appropriate to conclude that 1st Corinthians 12:13 also describes a baptism "with" or "in" the Holy Spirit administered by Christ.

temple in the Lord" (Eph. 2:21). However, the obvious question still remains. Does this occurrence described in 1 Corinthians 12:13 also refer to water baptism? In other words, does Scripture discriminate between the indwelling of the Holy Spirit and water baptism?

What occurs, for example, during the only two events recorded in Acts that specifically refer to a "baptism with the Holy Spirit?" At Pentecost, the disciples who remained in the upper room were clearly baptized with the Holy Spirit and were indwelt by the Holy Spirit outside any exchange of water. So in our first example, the baptism with the Holy Spirit did not occur during water baptism. But most people have contended that this was an anomaly and not subject to common experience. I thoroughly agree with that interpretation, but if this is true, then the other example recorded in Acts should support Wheeler Robinson's and E.Y. Mullin's view. However, Peter explained something quite different at Jerusalem when he recalled the events that took place at Caesarea:

> "And I remembered the word of the Lord, how he said, 'John baptized with water, but you will be baptized with the Holy Spirit.' *If then God gave the same gift to them as he gave us when we believed in the Lord Jesus Christ,* who was I that I could stand in God's way?'" (Acts 11:16-17; *emphasis added*).

Here, we see Peter recall a "baptism with the Holy Spirit" and the indwelling of the Spirit (i.e. the gift referred to in the above text) that preceded water baptism.[42] It should also be noted that these events were distinguished both in time and experience. In fact, it was the effects that resulted from the baptism with the Holy Spirit that provided justification for Peter to baptize Cornelius in water (cf. Acts 10:44-48; Acts 15:8-9). In fewer words, it is the indwelling of the Spirit that permits and requires Cornelius to receive baptism, not the other way around.[43] This pattern evidently is the common pattern for the church. As Paul explained in his letter to the Ephesians, "In him you also, when you heard the word of truth, the gospel of your salvation, and believed in him, were sealed with the promised Holy Spirit" (Eph. 1:13; cf. Gal. 3:2, 5, 10; Rom. 5:1, 5; John 7:39; Acts 11:16-17; 15:8-9; 19:2). So, the baptism with the Holy Spirit and the indwelling of the Spirit must occur on initial faith in Christ which *precedes* water baptism. If the baptism with the Holy Spirit cannot be distinguished from water baptism, both events recorded in Acts don't exegetically support that conclusion.[44]

---

[42] There can be no doubt that Cornelius' baptism with the Spirit was his initiation into Christ (i.e. his conversion).

[43] Another example can be seen in Paul's conversion, where Paul is filled with the Holy Spirit and then baptized (Acts 9:17-18). In comparison to the parallel account, Paul comes to faith in Christ and is chosen to be a witness for God (Acts 26:12-18). The latter certainly implies that Paul was indwelt by the Spirit on initial faith (cf. Acts 1:8).

[44] The same could also be said regarding two other passages in Acts (Acts 8:16; 19:2, 6). The Samaritans, for example, had received both the gospel and Christian baptism, although they had not yet received the Holy Spirit. As Luke explains, "for He had not yet fall on any of them, but they had only been baptized in the name

Charles Ryrie makes an appropriate comment pertaining to this subject. He explains, "Overemphasis on water baptism, particularly by immersion, often obscures or even obliterates the doctrine of Spirit baptism. If the two truths are not distinguished, usually the truth of Spirit baptism gets lost, for it is regarded simply as another way of talking about water baptism."[45]

---

of the Lord Jesus" (Acts 8:16). At that point, Luke was careful to inform that the Samaritans had failed to receive the baptism with the Holy Spirit and consequently, the indwelling Spirit himself (cf. 1 Cor. 12:13). As John Stott observed, "Contrary to expectation, water baptism had been received without Spirit baptism, the sign without the thing signified." In Ephesus, Paul had questioned the former disciples of John; "Did you receive the Holy Spirit when you believed?" (Acts 19:2). His first question links the reception of the Spirit with initial faith. As David Williams explains, "This question implies that the Holy Spirit is received at a definite point in time and that the time is the moment of initial belief (the aorist participle, *pisteusantes,* being construed here as coincidental to the verb, *elabete).* The same thought is expressed, for example, in Ephesians 1:13: "In him you also, when you heard the word of truth, the gospel of your salvation, and believed in him, were sealed with the promised Holy Spirit." (*New International Biblical Commentary: Acts.* Peabody: Hendrickson, 1990). (p. 329). Paul's second question demonstrates that the sign (water baptism) must have involved an understanding of the Spirit's indwelling (the thing signified): "Unto what then were you baptized?" (Acts 19:3). But more important to our argument, even when these disciples believed and received baptism, the Spirit's reception was once again delayed. The point is there was a distinction between Spirit baptism and water baptism, even in both abnormal cases.
[45] Ryrie, Charles C. *Basic Theology: A Popular Systematic Guide to Understanding Biblical Truth.* Chicago: Moody Publishers, 1991. (Kindle Location 6841). Kindle Edition.

The Effects of Spirit Baptism

What exactly are the effects of the baptism with the Holy Spirit? In response, Spirit baptism vitally unites souls as "one body in Christ, and individually members one of another" (Rom. 12:5). Christianity is not merely a religion where people believe in certain facts. It is a relationship in which there is a real union between the Lord Jesus Christ and the individual. As MacArthur observes, "Spirit baptism brings the believer into a vital union with Christ. To be baptized with the Holy Spirit means that Christ immerses us in the Spirit, thereby giving us a common life principle. This spiritual baptism is what connects us with all other believers in Christ and makes us part of Christ's own body. Baptism with the Spirit makes all believers one."[46] This is yet another reason why water baptism must be distinguished from the baptism with the Holy Spirit. For many who receive water baptism are neither spiritually united with Christ nor do they possess His indwelling Spirit (see the case of Simon in Acts 8:14-24). And these two concepts, unity with Christ and the Spirit's indwelling, are always interrelated. "And I will ask the Father, and he will give you another Helper, to be with you forever, even the Spirit of truth, whom the world cannot receive, because it neither sees him nor knows him. You know him, for he dwells with you and will be in you. In that day you will know that I am in my Father, and you in me, and I in you" (John 14:16-17, 20; cf. 1 Cor. 12:13; Rom. 8:9). Furthermore, to be united with Christ in his body

---

[46] MacArthur, John. *Charismatic Chaos*. Grand Rapids: Zondervan Publishing House, 1991. (p. 189).

indicates that our penalty to the Law has been satisfied since "He himself bore our sins in his body on the tree, that we might [also] die to sin and live to righteousness" (1 Pet. 2:24). In other words, his death which satisfied God's wrath towards sin effectively became ours. In Galatians, Paul wrote, "For through the law I died to the law, so that I might live to God" (Gal. 2:19). But how exactly could this be true? How could Paul have experienced his death for sin which the Law of God demanded? He unfolds the answer in his next statement: "I have been crucified with Christ, It is no longer I who live, but Christ who lives in me. And the life I live I live *by faith* in the Son of God" (Gal. 2:20; *emphasis added*). As MacArthur points out, "We were not physically at the crucifixion when Christ died, but as believers we willingly accept the truth that, *by faith*, we died with Him. We did not literally enter the grave with Christ and were not literally resurrected with Him, but *by faith* we were accounted to have been buried and raised with Him."[47] Christian baptism, then, is a visible witness to the believer's unity with Christ and the indwelling of the Holy Spirit.[48] However, for baptism to genuinely function as a witness to one's union with Christ and the Spirit's indwelling, the one baptized must

---

[47] MacArthur, John. *Romans 1-8: The MacArthur New Testament Commentary: Macarthur New Testament Commentary Series.* Chicago: Moody Publishers, 1991. (Kind Location 6779). Kindle Edition.

[48] It should be noted here that Christian baptism administered by immersion is the only form of baptism that provides the visible witness of dying to the old life and being raised to new life in Christ. This will be discussed more thoroughly in a later chapter.

have already experienced by faith the reality which water baptism illustrates.

The Charismatic Response

The majority of Charismatics and Pentecostals believe Spirit baptism is the first experience of the Spirit's empowering work that inaugurates a life characterized by continued anointing with the Spirit.[49] However, they do not view this as an experience reserved for all members of the church. In other words, they believe that the baptism with the Holy Spirit is available to all Christians, but they concede not every Christian will actually experience this event. Furthermore, their position believes that the initial evidence of Spirit baptism is speaking in tongues. In fact, Douglas Oss argues, "If there is no manifestation of tongues, then there has been no Spirit-baptism."[50] Their argument stems from the pattern illustrated in the Book of Acts (see Acts 2:1-3; 8:4-35; Acts 10:43-48, cf. Acts 11:16-17; Acts 19:1-7). That is, Acts consistently portrays speaking in tongues as the manifestation that accompanies Spirit baptism. Notably, their position does not suggest the Holy Spirit does not indwell believers. In fact, Charismatics will further characterize the indwelling of the Spirit as an unqualified experience reserved for all Christians (cf. Rom. 8:9). However, to discriminate between these two events (indwelling and empowerment),

---

[49] Grudem, Wayne. *Are Miraculous Gifts for Today?* Grand Rapids: Zondervan Publishing House, 1996. (p. 243).

[50] Grudem, Wayne. *Are Miraculous Gifts for Today?* Grand Rapids: Zondervan Publishing House, 1996. (p. 260).

Charismatics interpret that 1st Corinthians 12:13 describes a baptism *"by the Holy Spirit"* which cannot be identical to a baptism *"with the Holy Spirit."* According to their understanding, the passage describes Spirit indwelling but not special enablement. In summary, Charismatics uphold that every Christian receives the resident Holy Spirit, but not every Christian will experience a "baptism with the Holy Spirit" which, according to their view, empowers them for a specific future service in the ministry.

First, it's important to address the Charismatic interpretation of 1st Corinthians 12:13. 1st Corinthians 12:13 generally opens with this phrase; "For by one Spirit." As MacArthur notes, "this is where much of the Charismatic confusion begins."[51] Ironically, the majority of the confusion stems from the translation of the single preposition *en.* In one of his earlier works, MacArthur made this comment:

> "This term *'en'* can be translated 'at,' 'by,' or 'with' – and some scholars might even translate it 'in.' Greek prepositions are translated differently depending on the case endings of the words that follow the prepositions. An accurate translation in 1st Corinthians 12:13, the most consistent in the context of the New Testament, would use either *by* or *with.* In other words, [as the passage explains] we are baptized *by* or *with* the Holy Spirit. [However], this must not be taken to mean that the Holy Spirit is the One

---

[51] MacArthur, John. *Charismatic Chaos.* Grand Rapids: Zondervan Publishing House, 1991. (p. 189).

who does the baptizing. Nowhere in the Bible is the Holy Spirit spoken of as the baptizer."[52]

As I mentioned earlier, if 1st Corinthians 12:13 does refer to Spirit baptism, then all members of the body have experienced this at their conversion. As Grudhem argues, "the baptism in the Holy Spirit, must refer to the activity of the Holy Spirit at the beginning of the Christian life when he gives us new spiritual life (*in regeneration*) and cleanses us and gives us a clear break with the power and love of sin (*the initial stage of sanctification*)"[53] Simply stated, to argue that the baptism with the Holy Spirit occurs sometime after one's conversion, suggests that salvation offered in Christ does not supply the Christian with all the essentials one needs for his or her spiritual service. If the Christian truly is complete in Christ, then being in Christ should mean the Christian lacks nothing (Col. 2:10; 2 Peter 1:2-3). Therefore, it is my conviction that Scripture instructs believers not to seek a "second experience" of empowerment which the Charismatics label as a "baptism with the Holy Spirit." Instead, Scripture instructs Christians to only yield, by faith, to the resources they already possess, leaning on God who supplies our strength (Eph. 5:18; 1 Peter 4:11).

But what about the events recorded in Acts? The Charismatic position does make a reasonable argument. Speaking in tongues does appear to be the common

---

[52] MacArthur, John. *Charismatic Chaos*. Grand Rapids: Zondervan Publishing House, 1991. (p. 189).
[53] Grudem, Wayne. *Systematic Theology: An Introduction to Biblical Doctrine*. Zondervan, 2009. (p. 768). Kindle Edition.

manifestation which accompanies the baptism with the Holy Spirit. In Acts 2, it is equally true that those who were already saved experienced a baptism with the Holy Spirit after their conversion (Acts 2:1-3; cf. Luke 10:20; John 6:44, 15:3; Matt. 16:16-17). However, it's inappropriate to suggest these disciples were indwelt by the Holy Spirit prior to Pentecost.[54] As MacArthur observes, "More than a week after Jesus breathed on them and promised the Spirit, the disciples had not gone anywhere or done anything that would manifest the Spirit's power and presence (cf. John 20:26)."[55] The first baptism with the Holy Spirit is actually detailed in Acts 2:1-3:

> "When the day of Pentecost arrived, they were all together in one place. And suddenly there came from heaven a sound like a mighty rushing wind, and it filled the entire house where they were sitting. And divided tongues as of fire appeared on them and rested on each one of them."

---

[54] Charismatics interpret that John 20:21-22 suggests that the disciples had already received the indwelling of the Holy Spirit. However, in light of other passages it is clear that the promise of the Spirit (i.e. his indwelling presence; cf. John 14:16-17) had not come to fulfillment until Jesus returned to the Father (Acts 2:33; Eph. 4:8; John 7:39, John 15:26; 16:7). In other words, the event described in John 20:21-22 should be viewed as a pledge. To put it plainly, the imperative, "Receive the Holy Spirit!" should be understood as having future reference, which is not abnormal in John's gospel.

[55] MacArthur, John. *Charismatic Chaos*. Grand Rapids: Zondervan Publishing House, 1991. (p. 176).

These disciples were then "filled with the Holy Spirit and [as a result] they began to speak in other languages as the Spirit gave them utterance" (Acts 1:4). In Paul's first letter to the church at Corinth, he explained how spiritual gifts are appropriated to the various members of the church. He informed his readers that all Christians (whether Jew or Greek) have been baptized in one Spirit into the body of Christ just as they all have received the indwelling Holy Spirit (1 Cor. 12:13). In fact, he explained all gifts are empowered by the Spirit who "apportions to each one individually as he wills" (see 1 Cor. 12:11, 30). And even though Paul clarified that all Christians experience this baptism in one Spirit, he also clearly implied that not all Christians would speak in tongues (cf. 1 Cor. 12:30). In other words, the speaking in tongues recorded in Acts appear to be a visible and audible testimony. This, in turn, led others to immediately conclude that the baptism with the Holy Spirit (i.e. incorporation into the body of Christ) had occurred. For example, those "from the circumcision who had come with Peter were amazed, because the gift of the Holy Spirit was poured out even on the Gentiles. For they were hearing them speaking in tongues and extolling God" (Acts 10:45-46; cf. Acts 11:16-17). It's apparent that the Jews at Caesarea were surprised that Gentiles could receive the fullness of the blessings they too had received. On a similar note, referring to the Samaritans, Grudem makes this observation:

> "When we see the delayed reception of the Spirit in Acts 8:4-24 (*note that a direct reference to Spirit baptism is not mentioned in this passage*), it's apparent that God in his

providence, sovereignly waited to give the new covenant reception and empowering of the Holy Spirit to the Samaritans directly through the hands of the apostles so that it might be evident to the highest leadership in Jerusalem church that Samaritans were not some second-class citizens but full members of the church. This was important because of the historical animosity between Jews and Samaritans."[56]

This pattern, however, is not the pattern of common experience for the church. Like Pentecost, this was a special event which occurred in a transitional period in redemptive history. As the day of Pentecost was the point of transition between the old and new covenant work of the Spirit, so was the event recorded in Acts 8. However, this was a transition between old animosity and the new unity required in the body of Christ. The same could essentially be said for the events recorded in Acts 19:1-8.[57] When we recall the events of Acts 10, however, the

---

[56] Grudem, Wayne. *Systematic Theology: An Introduction to Biblical Doctrine.* Zondervan, 2009. (p. 773). Kindle Edition.

[57] Paul's question in Acts 19:2 is imperative to our understanding on this subject. Paul asks, "Did you receive the Holy Spirit when you believed?" This passage implies, once again, that the Spirit's reception is at a definite point in time and predicated on initial faith. As David Williams points out that the aorist participle, *pisteusantes,* should be construed here as coincidental with the verb, *elate* (*New International Biblical Commentary: Acts* [Peabody, Mass.: Hendrickson, 1990], 329). The reception of the Spirit on this occurrence was one again manifested with the speaking of tongues. This pattern, by God's sovereign choice,

pattern is more typical for the Christian. We observe that no time interval passed between faith and the indwelling of the Holy Spirit. However, the gift of tongues which accompanied this ordeal seems to be a rare repetition of the miraculous to demonstrate once again that God showed no partiality between Jews and Greeks, having thus incorporated Cornelius and his family into the body of Christ. In fact, Peter may not have accepted their faith as genuine if there was not some display of the Spirit's indwelling.

The Book of Acts clearly serves as a book of transition. Consequently, there are certainly a number of things which occur throughout Acts that are simply not common. As these events occurred, the canon of the New Testament was literally being written to form our understanding of the salvation offered in Christ. So when we carefully observe the other writings of the New Testament, we learn how to better interpret the events recorded in Luke's second account.

The Church of Christ Response

Everett Ferguson, who represents the Church of Christ position, equates the baptism with the Holy Spirit to speaking in foreign languages. However, he indicated that speaking in foreign languages "served to provide divine authorization for the proclamation and spread of the gospel and of the incorporation of all peoples into the church of

---

once again seems to provide visible and audible evidence to the apostles that all peoples are being incorporated into the church through the prevalent gospel of Jesus Christ.

Christ."[58] In other words, Ferguson does not associate the baptism with the Holy Spirit with one's conversion, but something essentially leading up to it. However, this definition is certainly inaccurate. The miraculous effects that resulted from the baptism with the Holy Spirit, for all intents and purposes, provided evidence that spiritual regeneration had already taken place, not the other way around (cf. Acts 11:16-18; cf. Acts 15:7-9). After all, the miraculous ability to speak in foreign languages in the New Testament was reserved specifically for members of the church (1 Cor. 12:4-11). Ferguson would also argue the baptism with the Holy Spirit is not a universal experience reserved for all Christians. He would appeal to Ephesians 4:5 which reads, "one Lord, one faith, one baptism." His argument would be this: "How can there currently be two baptisms for the Christian (i.e. the baptism with the Holy Spirit and water baptism), if Paul indicated there is only one baptism?" His position presumes the "one baptism" refers to water baptism. In his logic, because the events recorded in Acts occurred prior to Paul's letter to the Ephesians, the baptism with the Holy Spirit (which he simply equates with speaking in tongues) must have ceased by the time Paul wrote his epistle. After all, Paul did explain to the Corinthians at some point speaking in tongues would cease (1 Cor. 13:8). This obviously is where his view deviates from the Charismatic position.

In response, one must recall that John's gospel did

---

[58] Ferguson, Everett. *Baptism in the Early Church: History, Theology, and Liturgy in the First Five Centuries.* Grand Rapids: Wm. B. Eerdmans Publishing Company, 2009. (pp. 183-184). Kindle Edition.

not refer to the baptism with the Holy Spirit in a future sense like the other Gospels. Instead, his reference takes the form of a present participle: "I myself did not know him, but he who sent me to baptize with water said to me, 'He on whom you see the Spirit descend and remain, this is he who *baptizes* with the Holy Spirit'" (John 1:33; *italics added*). Why is this important? To put it plainly, the use of a present participle designates an unending or timeless action. In other words, the baptism with the Holy Spirit doesn't just describe the transitional events recorded in Acts, but it describes the distinct and continuing ministry of Jesus Christ. John assured his readers that Jesus would be known, without interruption, as the one who baptizes with (or in) the Holy Spirit. This understanding only gains further support from the parallel text in this same passage; "The next day he saw Jesus coming toward him, and said, 'Behold, the Lamb of God, who *takes away* the sin of the world'" (John 1:29; *italics added*)! Here John uses another present participle (*ho airōn*) to clarify his point. In other words, the reader should comprehend the ministry of Jesus Christ as being twofold. Not only does Christ remove sin from those who believe (negative), but he also baptizes with the Holy Spirit (positive). Both of these features were future in comparison to the ministry of John the Baptist. For example, Jesus could not take away sins (i.e. make propitiation) until his actual death on the cross, and neither could he baptize with the Holy Spirit until returning to the Father (cf. John 16:7). However, John's use of present participles infers that Jesus Christ will continuously be known as the one who not only takes away sin, but the one who also baptizes with the Holy Spirit (cf. Rom. 8:9). John

60

Stott adds this note; "As John was notoriously known as 'the baptizer' because it was characteristic of his ministry to baptize with water, so Jesus could be called 'the baptizer' because it would be characteristic of his ministry to baptize with the Holy Spirit."[59] If the baptism with the Holy Spirit had in fact ceased (which is what Ferguson believes), then why would John use a verb tense that designates timeless action? In response, he would not.[60] I would agree, however, that the "one baptism" does refer to water baptism in Ephesians 4:5. As Paul uses the words Lord and faith in their literal sense, so he uses the word baptism in its literal sense. In this regard, there is but one baptism.[61] Earlier, John the Baptist foretold that Christ would baptize with the Holy Spirit. On another occasion, Jesus had even told his disciples that they would receive a baptism that related to his suffering (Mark 10:38; Luke 12:50). These, of course, were not literal baptisms, but figurative. Furthermore, it's apparent that these two baptisms (i.e. Spirit baptism and baptism of suffering) did not refer to the same occurrence or to water baptism for that matter. More importantly, they extended to the members of the church.[62] However, there is

---

[59] Stott, John. *Baptism and Fullness.* Downers Gove, Illinois: InterVarsity Press, 2006. (p. 31).

[60] It's important to note the gospel of John was written in approximately 80 A.D., well after the book of Ephesians was written by the apostle Paul.

[61] Dagg, J.L. (2010-07-07). *Manual of Theology Second Part: A Treatise on Church Order.* Sprinkle Publications, 1982. (Kindle Location 137). Kindle Edition.

[62] As I have already explained in the present chapter, the baptism with the Holy Spirit is a universal experience for believers of the church. The reference to suffering in Mark 10:38 and Luke 12:15

only one literal baptism to be administered in water. Since baptism logically and chronologically follows faith, it would seem best to interpret the "one baptism" in Ephesians 4:5 as referring to water baptism. However, this in no way suggests the baptism with the Holy Spirit had ceased or that it is identical to water baptism. As Paul informed, we must rightly divide the word of truth (cf. 2 Tim. 2:15).

Summary

Although, this doctrine has historically divided Christians, I hope that some readers can appreciate what I have shared. The baptism with the Holy Spirit incorporates believers into the body of Christ at conversion. This originated at Pentecost when the baptizing work with the Holy Spirit actually began. From this point forward, all true members of the church would not only be baptized "in one Spirit," but they would also receive the Holy Spirit's indwelling (1 Cor. 12:13). Christian baptism, then, is a visible witness to this baptism (cf. Acts 10:44-48). It would immediately follow initial faith in Christ which is where these other events are said to have occurred. Although the two baptisms are interrelated, they are not identical. One is the sign (water), while the other is the thing signified (the Spirit). Irrespective, neither one has lost its proper importance for the church.

---

most likely referred to the suffering or death the apostles would later experience. But being willing to suffer for the sake of Christ defines any true Christian (cf. Luke 14:27; 2 Tim. 3:12). It would be difficult, then, to suggest this baptism of suffering, albeit figurative, was not reserved for believers in the church as well.

Christian Baptism

In the present chapter, I hope to explain both the meaning and importance of Christian baptism. And to do this, we begin with the closing words of Matthew's gospel. "And Jesus came and said to them, 'All authority in heaven and on earth has been given to me. Go therefore and make disciples of all nations, baptizing them in the name of the Father and of the Son and of the Holy Spirit, teaching them to observe all that I have commanded you. And behold, I am with you always, to the end of the age" (Matt. 28:18-20). As most of us are fully aware, this passage has historically been labeled as the *Great Commission*. However, in order to fully understand the relevance of this passage, one must first understand the relationship baptism had to our Lord's earthly ministry. Ironically, the Synoptics are silent regarding the baptisms authorized by Jesus and his disciples.[63] The gospel of John, however, does briefly account for this portion of his ministry (cf. John 3:22-26; 4:1). As Murray explains, "John's account implies that there was a period when the ministries of John and Jesus were exercised concurrently, and somewhat surprisingly, that the baptizing ministry of Jesus was more successful than that of his forerunner."[64] In reality this should not have come as a surprise. At least it did not for John the Baptist. He informed his followers, "He must increase, but I must decrease" (John 3:30). So the baptisms initially authorized by Jesus appear to be temporary in nature. Christ would authorize a baptism identical to John's, which would serve as a transition to his own ministry. By doing this he would also acknowledge the validity of John's ministry as the forerunner of Messiah. However, these baptisms initially authorized by Jesus apparently stopped. Since the Synoptics fail to even mention the baptizing ministry of Jesus, most commentators have agreed that it was actually limited to the earliest portion of his ministry.[65] In other words, it appears that Jesus refrained from permitting his disciples to baptize during the latter part of his earthly ministry. So what had taken

[63] As I mentioned in the chapter concerning John's baptism, Jesus did not personally baptize anyone but authorized his disciples to administer baptism (cf. John 4:2).

[64] Murray-Beasley, G.R. *Baptism in the New Testament*. Grand Rapids: William B. Eerdman's Publishing Company, 1962/1973. (p. 67).

[65] As Murray notes, this would have occurred prior to John's imprisonment and in the area south of Galilee, since the Synoptics do not account for the activities of Jesus prior to his Galilean ministry.

place to cause our Lord to delegate this instruction to baptize going forward? Many thoughts could obviously be said in response to that question. However, one thing is for certain. As a result of Israel's unbelief and rejection of their Messiah, God would make a significant change in the progression of redemptive history (cf. Luke 19:41; Matt. 23:37-39). God would temporarily set aside Israel and call out a new people for His name and purpose. Gentiles, who were once considered "alienated from the commonwealth of Israel," would now be engrafted with believing Jews into one body, the church (Eph. 2:12). Now this actually began on the Day of Pentecost following our Lord's resurrection. In fact, Pentecost marks the beginning of the church as a functioning body when the baptizing work with the Holy Spirit began (cf. Acts 2:1-3; 11:15-18). It's further evident that the instruction given by our Lord to baptize would not take effect until the church was in operation. For example, the first water baptisms recorded in Scripture following our Lord's instruction occurred after Peter's Sermon at Pentecost. "So those who received his word were baptized, and there were added that day about three thousand souls" (Acts 2:41). From this point forward, the church would consist of an assembly of believers in Christ, whether Jew or Greek, who have been baptized in water by immersion. As Ryrie observes, "Without debating the mode of baptism, it is clear that the New Testament knows nothing of unbaptized church members."[66] Baptism, then, would be an act of obedience. That is, all those who have

---

[66] Ryrie, Charles C. *Basic Theology: A Popular Systematic Guide to Understanding Biblical Truth.* Chicago: Moody Publishers, 1991. (Kindle Locations 7684-7685). Kindle Edition.

trusted in the Lord Jesus Christ for salvation are required to receive baptism following their exercise of belief. The following examples recorded in Scripture plainly support this conclusion:

> Whoever believes and is baptized will be saved, but whoever does not believe will be condemned (Mark 16:16).

> Peter said to them, "Repent and be baptized every one of you in the name of Jesus Christ for the forgiveness of your sins, and you will receive the gift of the Holy Spirit. For the promise is for you and for your children and for all who are far off, everyone whom the Lord our God calls to himself" (Acts. 2:38-39).

> "So those who received his word were baptized, and there were added that day about three thousand souls. And all who believed were together and had all things in common" (Acts 2:41, 44).

> "But when they believed Philip as he preached good news about the kingdom of God and the name of Jesus Christ, they were baptized, both men and women (Acts 8:12).

> And the eunuch said to Philip, "About whom, I ask you, does the prophet say this, about himself or about someone else?" Then Philip opened his mouth, and beginning with the Scripture he told him the good news about

Jesus. And as they were going along the road they came to some water, and the eunuch said, "See, here is water! What prevents me from being baptized?" And he commanded the chariot to stop, and they both went down into the water, Philip and the eunuch and he baptized him (Acts 8:34-38).[67]

"To him all the prophets bear witness that everyone who believes in him receives the forgiveness of sins." While Peter was still saying these things, the Holy Spirit fell on all who heard the word. Then Peter declared, "Can anyone withhold water for baptizing these people, who have received the Holy Spirit just as we have?" And he commanded them to be baptized in the name of Jesus Christ (Acts 10:43-44, 47-48).

One who heard us was a woman named Lydia, from the city of Thyatira, a seller of purple goods, who was a worshiper of God. The Lord opened her heart to pay attention to what was said by Paul. And after she was baptized, and her household as well, she urged us, saying, "If you have judged me to be faithful to the Lord, come to my house and stay." And she prevailed upon us (Acts 16:14-15).

---

[67] Although faith is not specifically mentioned, the author anticipates his readers to assume that the eunuch's hearing of the gospel message and his request to be baptized implies that he believed in Jesus.

Then he brought them out and said, "Sirs, what must I do to be saved?" And they said, "Believe in the Lord Jesus, and you will be saved, you and your household." And they spoke the word of the Lord to him and to all who were in his house. And he took them the same hour of the night and washed their wounds; and he was baptized at once, he and all his family (Acts 16:30-33).

Crispus, the ruler of the synagogue, believed in the Lord, together with his entire household. And many of the Corinthians hearing Paul believed and were baptized (Acts 18:8).

And he said, "Into what then were you baptized?" They said, "Into John's baptism." And Paul said, "John baptized with the baptism of repentance, telling the people to believe in the one who was to come after him, that is Jesus." On hearing this, they were baptized in the name of the Lord Jesus (Acts 19:3-5).

The normal reading of these passages clarifies that belief precedes and grounds the legitimacy of Christian baptism. In other words, baptism is appropriately administered only to those who provide a credible profession of faith in Christ.

The Mode of Christian Baptism

Baptism, in its New Testament context, is always administered by immersion. That is, the person being baptized is put completely under water and is subsequently raised out of the water. As I already explained in a previous chapter, the recipients of John's baptism were completely immersed (cf. Mark 1:5, 10; John 3:23). Those who would later receive Christian baptism would follow the same pattern. For example, after Philip had shared the gospel with the Ethiopian eunuch, both men went *"down into the water,* Philip and the eunuch, and he baptized him. And when they came *up out of the water,* the Spirit of the Lord carried Philip away, and the eunuch saw him no more, and went on his way rejoicing" (Acts 8:38-39; *emphasis added*). Baptism by immersion is the only suitable explanation of this passage. Unfortunately, other examples like this pertaining to Christian baptism are not widespread throughout the New Testament. But as many scholars have pointed out, the very word *baptizo* means to plunge, dip, or immerse something in or under water. Furthermore, it should be noted that the word *baptizo* is never used in a passive voice with water relating to its subject.[68] In other words, water is never said to be baptized on someone. Just the opposite, those who are baptized are immersed into or under water. In fact, there is no passage in the New Testament that would suggest the contrary to be true. Neither is there any sufficient reason to believe

---

[68] Strong, Augustus. *Systematic Theology: A Compendium and Commonplace-Book Designed for the Use of Theological Students.* Wentworth Press, 2011. (Kindle Location 43885). Kindle Edition

any New Testament author attached a different meaning to baptism besides that of immersion.

The Relationship between Baptism and the Holy Spirit

Although there is continuity between the redeemed of all stages in human history, there is a discontinuity between those who are currently being redeemed under the church age and those redeemed prior to its establishment. As Ryrie contends, "The church stands unique in the purposes of God. Although God has related Himself to other groups, His activity with the church remains distinct."[69] In fact, the New Testament makes clear on several different occasions that members of Christ's body would participate in blessings that others did not experience earlier in history. For example, one major distinction between those groups and the church is the relation of the church to the indwelling Holy Spirit. From Pentecost forward, *all* genuine Christians would receive the indwelling Holy Spirit (cf. Rom. 8:9; John 7:39; 14:17). The Holy Spirit would not only empower believers for Christian service, but he would also provide them with spiritual gifts necessary to accomplish God's will. As we study the New Testament, it's evident that the indwelling of the Holy Spirit and water baptism would be intimately related. The Book of Acts makes this clear on several occurrences. For example, there are

---

[69] Ryrie, Charles C. *Basic Theology: A Popular Systematic Guide to Understanding Biblical Truth.* Chicago: Moody Publishers, 1991. (Kindle Locations 7514-7515). Kindle Edition.

times recorded in Acts where baptism is actually said to precede the reception of the Spirit. "Repent and be baptized every one of you in the name of Jesus Christ for the forgiveness of your sins, and you will receive the gift of the Holy Spirit" (Acts 2:38). In the instance of Cornelius, however, it must be observed that the indwelling of the Spirit actually preceded water baptism. When Peter recalled this event in Jerusalem, he said, "who was I that I could stand in God's way" (Acts 11:17). This refers back to his earlier statement made at Caesarea; "Can anyone withhold water for baptizing these people, who have [already] received the Holy Spirit just as we have?" (Acts 10:47). As Robert H. Stein observes, "It is the reception of the Spirit that permits and requires Cornelius to be baptized."[70] It should further be noted that Peter testified of this once more at the Jerusalem Council (Acts 15:7-10). Then, of course, there are other occurrences recorded in Acts which do not stringently follow either of the two previous patterns (cf. Acts 8:12, 14-17; Acts 19:5-6). So how should we interpret the relationship between the indwelling of the Spirit and water baptism having seen the variations recorded in Acts? In response, Acts presents a transitional period where God's focus turns from Israel to the church. Consequently, the events recorded in Acts are not always normative to common experience. However, the New Testament consistently teaches that the gift of the Holy Spirit is received upon initial faith in Christ.

---

[70] Schreiner, T., & Wright, Shawn. *Believer's Baptism*. B & H Publishing Group, 2006. (p. 62). Nook Edition.

"Now this he said about the Spirit, whom those who had believed in him were to receive, for as yet the Spirit has not been given, because Jesus was not yet glorified" (John 7:39).

"And I remembered the word of the Lord, how he said, 'John baptized with water, but you will be baptized with the Holy Spirit.' If then God gave the same gift to them as he gave us when we believed in the Lord Jesus Christ, who was I that I could stand in God's way" (Acts 11:16-17)?

"And after there had been much debate, Peter stood up and said to them, 'Brothers, you know that in the early days God made a choice among you, that by my mouth the Gentiles should hear the word of the gospel and believe. And God, who knows the heart, bore witness to them, by giving them the Holy Spirit just as he did to us, and he made no distinction between us and them, having cleansed their hearts by faith'" (Acts 15:7-10).

"And he said to them, 'Did you receive the Holy Spirit when you believed'" (Acts 19:2).

"Let me ask you only this: 'Did you receive the Spirit by works of the law or by hearing with faith?'" (Gal. 3:2).

"Does he who supplies the Spirit to you and works miracles among you do so by works of the law, or by hearing with faith – just as

Abraham believed God, and it was counted to him as righteousness?" (Gal. 3:5).

"So that in Christ Jesus the blessing of Abraham might come to the Gentiles, so that we might receive the promised Spirit through faith" (Gal. 3:14).

"For through the Spirit, by faith, we ourselves eagerly wait for the hope of righteousness" (Gal. 5:5).

"Therefore, since we have been justified by faith, we have peace with God through our Lord Jesus Christ. God's love has been poured into our hearts through the Holy Spirit who has been given to us" (Rom. 5:1, 5).

"In him you also, when you heard the word of truth, the gospel of your salvation, and believed in him, were sealed with the promised Holy Spirit" (Eph. 1:13).

From the above passages, it's evident that the Spirit's indwelling is predicated on initial belief, not baptism. As Stein notes, "The association of baptism with the gift of the Spirit, while closely connected, is not portrayed as involving an automatic causal relationship."[71] But if that's true, then why do these two events appear so closely related throughout the New Testament? As I explained in the previous chapter, the Spirit's indwelling is predicated

---

[71] Schreiner, T., & Wright, Shawn. *Believer's Baptism.* B & H Publishing Group, 2006. (pp. 62-63). Nook Edition.

on unity with Christ or *vice versa* (cf. 1 Cor. 12:13; Rom. 8:9; John 14:16-17, 20). And if we are united with Christ we are said to participate in both his death and resurrection (cf. Rom. 6:5). One purpose of baptism is to visibly illustrate this spiritual reality. "Do you not know that all of us who have been baptized into Christ Jesus were baptized into his death? We were buried therefore with him by baptism into death, in order that, just as Christ was raised from the dead by the glory of the Father, we too might walk in newness of life" (Rom. 6:3-4). This is yet another reason why baptism must be by immersion. Evidently, when a person's body is submerged under the water during baptism, that act in itself pictures the death, burial, and resurrection of the believer. It is during this occasion that he or she personally identifies with the death and resurrection of Jesus Christ. As J.L. Dagg observes, "Water baptism, as a Christian rite, is not administered to cleanse the flesh, either literally or ceremonially. It figuratively represents the burial and resurrection of Christ, on which the believer relies for salvation."[72] Since baptism is so uniquely tied to one's unity with Christ and the indwelling of the Holy Spirit, it is imperative to understand that our biblical authors never separated water baptism from the overall experience of conversion. However, for baptism to truly function properly, the person receiving baptism must already be regenerate having believed in the Lord Jesus Christ. Consequently, an appropriate tension must be held. In his commentary

---

[72] Dagg, J.L. (2010-07-07). *Manual of Theology Second Part: A Treatise on Church Order.* Sprinkle Publications, 1982. (Kindle Location 135). Kindle Edition.

on Paul's letter to the Colossians, Douglas Moo has made an appropriate observation:

> "Baptism does not symbolize what happened when we were converted; it somehow is integrally involved in that conversion itself. The best way to account for this and at the same time do justice to Paul's constant emphasis on our faith as the key to our coming to Christ is again to recognize a broadly attested New Testament theological concept dubbed by James Dunn 'conversion-initiation.' The New Testament connects our coming to Christ (being converted and being initiated into the new covenant community) to faith, to repentance, to the gift of the Spirit, and to water baptism, in various combinations. Any of these, in a kind of metonymy, could be used to connote the whole experience – implying, of course, in each instance, the presence of all the others. Water baptism, then, as a critical New Testament rite intimately connected to our conversion experience, could be used as shorthand for the whole experience."[73]

If churches would teach this truth about baptism more clearly, it would certainly receive a greater importance than what it currently does among evangelical circles.

---

[73] Moo, Douglas J. *The Letters to the Colossians and to Philemon (Pillar New Testament Commentary).* Grand Rapids: Wm. B. Eerdmans Publishing, 2008. (Kindle Location 3786). Kindle Edition.

The Relationship between Baptism and the Forgiveness of Sin

In Acts the forgiveness of sins is also associated with being baptized. At Pentecost, for example, Peter instructed the crowds to "Repent and be baptized every one of you in the name of Jesus Christ for the forgiveness of sins, and you will receive the gift of the Holy Spirit" (Acts 2:38). After recovering his sight, Paul was even told, "And now why do you wait? Rise and be baptized and wash away your sins, calling on his name" (Acts 22:16). As Wayne Grudem observes, "Sometimes it is objected that the essential thing symbolized in baptism is not death and resurrection with Christ but purification and cleansing from sins." He further adds, "Certainly it is true that water is an evident symbol of washing and purification from sins as well as death and resurrection with Christ."[74] Still, the cleansing and forgiveness of sin should not overshadow the emphasis placed on dying and rising with Christ in baptism. As Dagg suggests, "If the doctrine of the resurrection be taken from the Gospel, preaching is vain, and faith is vain. So, if the symbol of the resurrection be taken from baptism, its chief significancy is gone, and its adaptedness for the profession of faith in Christ, is lost."[75] Many, however, disagree that baptism is only a figure for the cleansing of sin. Instead they argue

---

[74] Grudem, Wayne. *Systematic Theology: An Introduction to Biblical Doctrine.* Zondervan, 2009. (p. 773). Kindle Edition.

[75] Dagg, J.L. (2010-07-07). *Manual of Theology Second Part: A Treatise on Church Order.* Sprinkle Publications, 1982. (Kindle Location 1045). Kindle Edition.

that baptism causally affects the forgiveness of sin, and by extension, spiritual salvation. However, it is equally true in the Book of Acts that forgiveness of sins was tied solely to repentance (cf. Acts 3:19; 5:31; 8:22; 11:18) and initial faith in Christ (cf. Acts 10:43; 13:39; 15:9; 16:31; 26:18). So, once again, a proper tension must be held. To suggest baptism affects spiritual salvation is to advocate that God has altered the way man appropriates salvation throughout the course of human history. However, Paul makes clear on several instances that God has never declared any person righteous on any other basis than by His grace through individual faith (cf. Rom. 4:1-8; 23-25). It is also clear from Paul's writing that God saves men apart from works or ritual (cf. Rom. 2:28-29; 4:9-12; Titus 3:5). Baptism would certainly be included in the latter category. Since Christian baptism always relates to those who have already repented from sin and have believed in Christ, then the forgiveness of sins must, in reality, precede water baptism. As Stein observes, "The account of the conversion of Cornelius (his receiving the gift of the Spirit [Acts 10:44-46] and his being baptized [Acts 10:47-48] is prefaced by the statement that everyone who believes in Jesus receives forgiveness of sins (Acts 10:43). Thus forgiveness of sins is a result of believing in Jesus, and the further consequence is that Cornelius received the gift of the Spirit and was baptized."[76] But if this is true, then how do we explain the few verses that seem to suggest baptism, in effect, yields the forgiveness of sin? How are we to account for those portions of Scripture? Despite the

---

[76] Schreiner, T., & Wright, Shawn. *Believer's Baptism*. B & H Publishing Group, 2006. (p. 65). Nook Edition.

fact that baptism visibly depicts the cleansing of sin, the first command for every believer is to receive baptism. This should be clearly understood not only from the *Great Commission* but also from the other examples recorded in Scripture (cf. Acts 2:41; 10:47-48; 16:31-33). And often times, this was a costly act of obedience to follow for the individual. Receiving baptism would essentially mark a public break with any other religious ties and require the believer to solely identify with the Lord Jesus Christ. This would certainly explain why the apostles sometimes included baptism in the call to conversion (cf. Acts 2:38). It would require many to forsake all in order to follow Christ (cf. Luke 14:33). As John MacArthur notes, "This would assume that every genuine believer would embark on a life of obedience and discipleship. That was nonnegotiable. Therefore the apostles viewed baptism as the turning point. Only those who were baptized were considered Christians."[77] In other words, the apostles often times associated water baptism with the forgiveness of sin because it visibly pictured the cleansing of sin and would further evidence the believer's willingness to obey our Lord's command despite what cost it could potentially have.

The Relationship between Baptism and Works

The gospel is a call to repent from sin and trust in the Lord Jesus Christ for salvation. Without the expression of both, there is no true conversion (cf. Acts 20:21).

---

[77] MacArthur John. *The Gospel According to the Apostles.* Nashville: Thomas Nelson, 2003 (p. 195). (Nook Edition).

Moreover, the Bible carefully explains that all men, without exception, cannot be justified by works (cf. Rom. 3:20, 28; 4:2, 4; 9:32; 11:6; Gal. 2:16; 3:2, 5; Eph. 2:8-10; 2 Tim. 1:9; Titus 3:5).[78] But what exactly are works? Although the works pertaining to the Mosaic Law are consistently referenced throughout Scripture, they need not be limited to this definition. As Paul informed in his letter to the Romans, "For if Abraham was justified by works, he has something to boast about, but not before God" (Rom. 4:2). Clearly the "works" referred to here are not works pertaining to the Mosaic Law, for the Law was not even in place at that particular time (cf. Gal. 3:15-18). With that being said, it is best to interpret works as things performed in our own human strength or through our natural human abilities. If Abraham could have been declared righteous through something he did in his own effort, then he indeed would have something to boast about in the presence of God. Yet, the Bible still affirms

---

[78] Many will argue that men are not saved by faith alone on the basis of James 2:24. However, if this were true then James would certainly contradict Paul's clear teaching on the nature of justification (cf. Rom. 3:20; 4:1-25; Gal. 3:6, 11). It should be observed that the works referred to in this passage was the offering up of Isaac which actually occurred several years after Abraham exercised faith and was declared righteous before God. This act of obedience, then, demonstrated the genuineness of his faith and the reality of his relationship to God. James seems to be illustrating that a person's salvation is evidenced in works, not merely in belief. Simply stated, without works there is no genuine claim to spiritual salvation. In fact, James' teaching actually complements Paul's teaching in every respect. Salvation is determined by God's grace through faith alone and demonstrated in man's obedience (cf. Eph. 2:8-10).

that "Abraham believed God, and it was counted to him as righteousness. For the one who works, his wages are not counted as a gift but as his due. And to the one who does not work, but believes in him who justifies the ungodly, his faith is counted as righteousness" (Rom. 4:4-5). So there is obviously a contrast between biblical faith and human works. But how is one to appropriately understand this contrast between the two? In response, faith, under its normal interpretation, is trusting in the Lord Jesus Christ for salvation having believed in both his death and resurrection. As many fail to acknowledge, biblical faith is not merely belief in an historical act. Biblical faith relies on Jesus Christ to eternally save the soul. It not only involves belief, but biblical faith also involves a heart of commitment. When a person truly believes in Jesus Christ, he is committing his life to our Savior's purpose and will. He affirms that Jesus Christ is Lord, and he willingly submits to our Lord's authority. As Paul explained, ""If you *confess with your mouth that Jesus is Lord* and believe in your heart that God raised him from the dead, you will be saved. For with the heart one believes and is justified, and with the mouth once confesses and is saved" (Rom. 10:9-10; *emphasis added*). Furthermore, initial faith also presumes the expression of repentance. As Berkhof observes, "Faith and repentance are distinct concepts, but they cannot occur independently of each other. Genuine repentance is *always* the flip side of faith; and true faith accompanies repentance."[79] Once again, this has always been God's requirements for spiritual salvation. God has never recognized any righteousness

---

[79] Berkhof, Louis. *Systematic Theology* (p.487).

but the righteousness which comes by faith (cf. Rom. 4:1-25; Gal. 3:1-29). But neither faith nor repentance can be accredited to man because within the saving work of God there is the creating of both repentance and faith necessary to receive the grace gift of salvation. Left to his own device, man could not procure such a response. As MacArthur notes, "Faith is not a meritorious work. It is never the ground for justification – it is simply the channel through which it is received and it, too, is a gift."[80] Notice, for example, the following texts recorded in Scripture:

> "But to all who did receive him, who believed in his name, he gave the right to become children of God who were born, *not of blood, nor of the will of the flesh, nor of the will of man, but of God*" (John 1:12-13; *emphasis added*).

> "For by grace have you been saved through faith. *And this is not your own doing; it is the gift of God,* not a result of works, so that no one may boast" (Eph. 2:8-9; *emphasis added*).

> "All things have been handed over to me by my Father, and no one knows the Son except the Father, and no one knows the Father except the Son and anyone to whom the Son *chooses to reveal him*" (Matt. 11:27; *emphasis added*).

---

[80] Macarthur, John. *ESV MacArthur Study Bible.* Good News Publishers/Crossway Books, 2010. (Kindle Locations 122542-122543). Kindle Edition.

> "Then to the Gentiles also *God has granted repentance that leads to life*" (Acts 11:18; *emphasis added*).

> "God, who saved us and called us to a holy calling, *not because of our works but because of his own purpose and grace, which he gave us in Christ Jesus before the ages began*" (2 Tim. 1:9; *emphasis added*)

> "He saved us, *not because of works done by us in righteousness, but according to his own mercy, by the washing of regeneration and renewal of the Holy Spirit*, whom he poured out on us richly through Jesus Christ our Savior, so that being justified by his grace we might become heirs according to hope of eternal life" (Titus 3:5-7; *emphasis added*).

From the above portions of Scripture, it's evident that man cannot accredit his salvation to anything that originates in him. As Paul wrote to the Corinthians, "God chose what is low and despised in the world, even the things that are not, to bring to nothing things that are, so that no human being might boast in the presence of God. *And because of him you are in Christ Jesus*, who became to us wisdom from God, righteousness and sanctification and redemption so that, as it is written, 'Let the one who boasts, boast in the Lord'" (1 Cor. 1:28-31; *emphasis added*). Again, repentance and faith are *all* that God requires to receive his gift of salvation. However, it is equally true that both are empowered by God's enabling. Consequently, all other human actions, by default, must be considered works. Since baptism is subsequent to initial faith and is furthermore distinct from it, then baptism must be labeled, like everything else, as a work that cannot result in spiritual salvation (cf. Eph. 2:9; Rom. 4:9-12). In fact, those who do not properly understand the tension held between baptism and spiritual salvation will actually be guilty of promoting a false gospel of human merit. Which, in reality, is no different than arguing a sinner's prayer is necessary for salvation. Like our biblical authors, we must conclude that no work is necessary for salvation which would certainly include the act of baptism. As Paul explained, "Christ did not send me to baptize but to preach the gospel, and not with words of eloquent wisdom, lest the cross of Christ be emptied of its power" (1 Cor. 1:17; cf. 1 Cor. 15:1-8, 11). The point is, even though baptism is a New Testament rite intimately related to one's conversion, it is not causal to spiritual salvation. Just the contrary, it is the evidence of it (cf. Eph. 2:8-10).

Summary

In conclusion, Christian baptism is a believer's baptism. It is an act of obedience for all those who have trusted in Christ for salvation to undergo in response to our Lord's command. As Scripture plainly informs, Christian baptism is connected with conversion. It is interrelated to our unity with Christ, the indwelling of the Holy Spirit, and the forgiveness of sin. With that being said, a proper tension must be held. Even though baptism is intimately tied to the experience of conversion, it does not affect spiritual salvation. For baptism to truly function properly in its New Testament framework, the person receiving baptism must already be regenerate. Unfortunately, the different views surrounding baptism have historically resulted in the failure to biblically carry out what Christ has commanded. We should be diligent with our Lord's instruction and strive to meet his demands as we further pursue his will and purpose.

Infant Baptism: Fact Or Fiction

In the previous chapter I endeavored to explain that Christian baptism is a believer's baptism, meaning it's reserved only for those who have exercised faith in Jesus Christ for salvation. This is the traditional credobaptist view on water baptism. Paedobaptists, however, hold to a different view. They believe water baptism should be performed through the act of sprinkling (not immersion) on the infants and small children of Christian adults. To complicate matters even further, we must notice the differences held among the groups who practice paedobaptism concerning what happens to the child when it is baptized. For example, the Roman Catholics and Lutheran church teach that baptism actually conveys salvation to the infant. Then there are certain groups such as the Presbyterian Church who teach that baptism is a covenant sign, much like that of physical circumcision, which cannot result in spiritual salvation but instead ushers them into the church community.

Even though infant baptism has been prevalent throughout church history, the practice of infant baptism lacks clear New Testament support. As mentioned in earlier chapters, there are prerequisites to receiving water baptism, namely repentance and faith (cf. Matt. 3:6; Mark 1:4-5, 16:16; Luke 3:12; Acts 2:38-41, 8:12, 8:36-38, 10:47, 13:24, 18:8, 19:4-5; Col. 2:12). In 1 Peter 3:21, Peter correlates baptism to "an appeal to God for a good conscience."[81] None of those realities – repentance, faith, or a conscious appeal to God for a good conscience – can be exhibited by an infant. So why does this argument even exist?

Advocates of infant baptism appeal to Acts 10, Acts 16, and 1 Corinthians 1 for proof that infant baptism is scriptural. Acts 10:24-48 provides the account of Cornelius and his "relatives and close friends" hearing the Gospel and being baptized. Acts 16 includes the baptism of Lydia's family and the Philippian jailer's family (cf. Acts 16:15, 33). In his letter to the Corinthians, Paul revealed that he baptized members related to the household of Stephanas (cf. 1 Cor. 1:16). In each of these occurrences, the proponents of infant baptism assume that there were children in the aforementioned households that were infants and that those infants received baptism.[82]

---

[81] Whether Peter is referring to water baptism or the spiritual reality water baptism symbolizes is irrelevant. See the exegesis section on 1 Peter 3:21 for additional comments.

[82] Lydia did not live in Philippi. She was from Thyatira, on the other side of the Aegean Sea. Since she was traveling, she

However, in each of these examples, those who were baptized were those who had received the gospel (cf. Acts 10:34-43; 16:14, 32; 1 Cor. 1:16-18; 16:15-16). They were those who could hear and understand the Word of God

---

probably did not bring her children with her, if she had any. In fact, the biblical account leads us to believe that Lydia's servants were baptized. Some still allege that Lydia's family members were baptized, not because they believed, but only because they were in Lydia's family. This allegation rests on the fact that Acts 16:14-15 denotes Lydia's belief, but does not specifically reveal that her family believed. However, the Bible clearly teaches that belief must precede baptism (cf. Mark 16:16; Acts 8:37; Rom. 10:10-11; 1 Cor. 1:21; Eph. 1:21), and that a sinner cannot be forgiven of sin based on the faith of another (cf. Matt. 12:36; Rom. 14:12; 1 Pet. 2:7; 4:5; 1 John 3:23). Furthermore, Acts 16:34 reports that the Philippian jailer's family was made up entirely of believers (excluding infants), and the accounts of both Cornelius' and the jailer's conversions specifically indicate that candidates for baptism were those who had "heard the word" (Acts 10:44,47). When inspired writers wrote about "hearing" the Word of God, "hearing" often denoted not only the recognition of audible sounds, of which infants are capable, but also understanding the message, of which infants are incapable (cf. Deut. 5:1; Rom. 10:17; Job 13:17; Luke 14:35). Some base their claim that infants of the jailer's household were baptized, upon the assumption that there would not have been enough water in a jail to immerse adults. Thus, they say, sprinkling was the mode of baptism, which would have been appropriate for infant baptism. However, Acts 16 suggests that Paul and Silas were not in the jail at the time of the major part of the teaching and the baptism, because they had been "brought out"—likely out of the prison itself—and taken to a place where the prisoners' stripes could be washed. It was at this place that the baptisms took place, so it is an imposition on the text to imply that Paul and Silas did not have access to enough water for immersion.

(cf. Acts 10:44), exercise faith, (cf. 10:31-33), and were able to serve in ministry (cf. 1 Cor. 16:15). The absence of the words repentance and faith in these biblical accounts certainly does not preclude them from being present in the historical account. Neither do these conversions demand that any infants were baptized. When our biblical authors referred to household baptisms it is best understood that the baptisms performed were limited to believers. To assert otherwise is to put an unnecessary strain on the biblical text. Even though well-respected bible teachers have taught that infant baptism is a biblical mode of baptism, a proper interpretation of Scripture will lead us to reject such notions.

The other side of this argument known as the "covenant" argument is more complex. Several groups argue that baptism is the New Testament counterpart to Old Testament circumcision. In the Old Testament, circumcision was administered to the male Israelite children as the outward sign of entrance into God's covenant community (cf. Gen. 17:10-14; Exod.12:43-49; Lev. 12:3). The parallel between baptism is derived from Colossians 2:11-12. "In him also you were circumcised with a circumcision made without hands, by putting off the body of the flesh, by the circumcision of Christ, having been buried with him in baptism, in which you were also raised with him through faith in the powerful working of God, who raised him from the dead." Paul evidently makes a connection between circumcision and baptism in this text. Those who support the "covenant" argument for infant baptism argue that baptism replaces the circumcision prescribed under the Old Covenant.

Therefore, baptism should be administered to the infants of believing parents. To deny infants this benefit would be to deny them an outward sign of entrance into God's covenant community.

To respond, the covenant community of Israel and the covenant community of our Lord's church are two very different things. To enter the covenant community of Israel, one had to have been born an Israelite and be circumcised on the eight day. The presence or absence of spiritual life made no difference (cf. Rom. 9:6). In the New Testament, however, those who receive baptism must provide testimony that they have believed in the gospel. In other words, they must provide evidence to their salvation experience. Paedobaptists fail to recognize this change from the way one participates in God's covenant community under each covenant. Under the Old Covenant (i.e. Israel), entrance into the covenant community was physical (circumcision). Under the New Covenant (i.e. the church), entrance into the covenant community is spiritual (salvation). Once again, a proper interpretation of Scripture will lead us to reject the practice of infant baptism.

Church Ordinance

The Lord Jesus gave the church two ordinances that they are to observe: baptism (Matt. 3:13-17; 28:19) and the celebration of the Lord's Supper (Luke 22:19-20). As mentioned in earlier chapters, Christian baptism is a believer's baptism. That is, all those who have trusted in Christ for salvation are required to receive baptism following their exercise of belief (cf. Matt. 16:16; Acts 2:38-41). Baptism then is a public profession of one's faith in Christ. Scripture suggests baptism should follow one's profession of faith as soon as reasonably possible (cf. Acts 2:41; 8:12; 8:38; 9:18; 10:48 18:8; 19:1-5). The mode of baptism is through the act of immersion. This means that the person being baptized should be put completely under the water and then brought back up again. While we recognize that Jesus commanded baptism (cf. Matt. 28:19), as did the apostles (cf. Acts 2:28), we should not say that baptism is a requirement for salvation. This does not mean that baptism is not closely related to conversion (cf. Acts 22:16). As Grudem accurately points out, "When baptism is properly carried out it brings spiritual benefit to believers. There is the blessing of God's favor that comes with all obedience, as well as the joy that comes through public profession of one's faith, and the reassurance of having a clear picture of dying and rising with Christ and of washing away sins."[83] Scripture does not specify any restrictions on who can perform baptism except that the person administering baptism must be a fellow believer in Christ. In general, church government calls for church officers or ordained ministers to perform this function. Although baptism can be performed in private or public settings, baptisms are generally administered in the presence of other local church members. Scripture does not require a certain formula or incantation to be said during baptism. However, on several different occasions, early church members were baptized specifically "in the name of the Lord Jesus" (cf. Acts 8:12, 16; 10:48; 19:5). Church tradition has led many to baptize in the name of Father, the Lord Jesus, and the Holy Spirit. Although this is not a biblical requirement, this practice does draw our attention to the Trinity. I personally agree with this practice as Scripture clearly indicates that each member of the Triune Godhead is involved in our salvation experience.

---

[83] Grudem, Wayne. *Systematic Theology: An Introduction to Biblical Doctrine.* Zondervan, 2009. (p. 980). Kindle Edition.

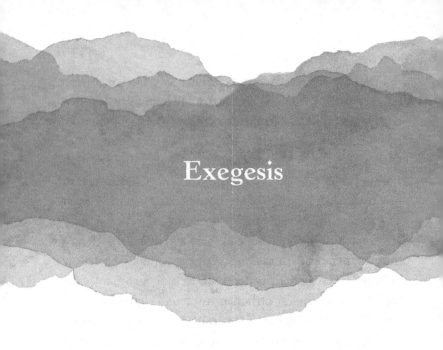

Exegesis

In the closing section of this book, we need to observe those passages of Scripture that have been used to support baptismal regeneration or salvation. God is not an author of confusion (cf. 1 Cor. 14:33). Neither does Scripture contradict itself. To say that baptism is necessary for salvation is to argue against the plain teaching of Scripture that salvation is received by faith alone. Therefore, there must be a different interpretation of those verses that seem to support baptismal salvation. Although a number of different resources exist which provide interpretations to the following passages, the following comments are a collection of my own personal thoughts and interpretations.

Mark 16:15-16

In the closing section of Mark's gospel, Jesus says, "Go into all the world and preach the gospel to all creation. He who has believed and has been baptized shall be saved; but he who has not believed shall be condemned" (Mark 16:15-16). There has always been a debate as to whether Mark 16:9-20 was originally part of the Gospel of Mark or whether a scribe added theses verses later. Some argue that we should not base a key doctrine on anything from Mark 16:9-20 unless it also supported by other passages of Scripture. However, let's assume Mark 16:9-20 is part of the original text and that it holds equal weight to all other recorded Scripture. What these verses teach is that belief is necessary for salvation, which is consistent with other portions of Scripture (cf. John 3:18, 5:24). "He who has not believed shall be condemned" (Mark 16:16). As I mentioned in an earlier chapter, the apostles sometimes included baptism in the call to conversion (cf. Acts 2:38). Still, they were careful to distinguish that salvation was applied through faith, not baptism (cf. Acts 15:8-10). It should not surprise us to hear similar words coming from our Lord (cf. Matt. 28:19). Water baptism was and still is a critical New Testament rite intimately connected to our conversion experience, and can be used to summarize the whole experience. Mark 16:15-16 clearly establishes that faith is required for salvation, but it does not prove that baptism is a requirement. Like the rest of Scripture, it simply argues that baptism is intimately connected to our overall conversion experience (cf. Acts 22:16).

John 3:5

During a conversation with Nicodemus, Jesus said, "Truly, truly, I say to you, unless one is born again he cannot see the kingdom of God" (John 3:3). Jesus elaborated on this concept further when he said, "Truly, truly, I say to you, unless one is born of water and the Spirit, he cannot enter the kingdom of God" (John 3:5). The phrase "born of water and the Spirit" has caused a great deal of confusion. If one thing is clear about this text, the topic on our Lord's mind is regeneration; the secret act of God where he imparts spiritual life to the believer. Consequently, proponents of baptismal salvation claim that "born of water" must refer to water baptism and state this text provides scriptural evidence for baptismal regeneration. However, if "born of water and the Spirit" does refer to water baptism, several questions should arise. For example, why would Jesus end this conversation with Nicodemus by demanding faith and not baptism? In fact, Jesus ended that conversation with these words: "As Moses lifted up the serpent in the wilderness, so must the Son of Man be lifted up, that whoever believes in him may have eternal life" (John 3:14). Scripture clearly indicates that regeneration is connected with the exercising of faith (cf. John 1: 12-13; 1 John 5:1). This section of Scripture is no different. So being "born of water and the Spirit" cannot refer to baptism. As many commentators are right to point out, the phrase "born of water and the Spirit" was given to provide clarification to Nicodemus. In other words, this phrase was supposed to tip off Nicodemus having been well studied in the Old Testament scriptures.

In the Old Testament, water and Spirit refer to spiritual cleansing and renewal (cf. Num. 19:17-19; Isa. 4:4; 32:15; 44:3; 55:1; Joel 2:28-29; Zech. 13:1). However, the most relevant passage is found in Ezekiel. "I will take you from the nations and gather you from all the countries and bring you into your own land. I will sprinkle clean water on you, and you shall be clean from all your uncleannesses, and from all your idols I will cleanse you. And I will give you a new heart, and a new spirit I will put within you. And I will remove the heart of stone from your flesh and give you a heart of flesh. And I will put my Spirit within you, and cause you to walk in my statutes and be careful to obey my rules" (Ezek. 36:24-27). As John MacArthur points out, "It was surely this passage that Jesus had in mind, showing regeneration to be an Old Testament truth (cf. Deut. 30:6; Jer. 31:31-34; Ezek. 11:18-20) with which Nicodemus would have been acquainted. Against the Old Testament backdrop, Christ's point was unmistakable: Without the Spiritual washing of the soul, a cleansing accomplished only by the Holy Spirit (Titus 3:5) through the Word of God (Eph. 5:26), no one can enter God's kingdom." [84]

Acts 2:38

Acts 2:38 has probably been used more than all other proof texts to support baptismal salvation. "And Peter said to them, 'Repent and be baptized every one

---

[84] MacArthur, John. *The MacArthur New Testament Commentary, Set of 30 Volumes.* Chicago: Moody Publishers. (Kindle Location 71041). Kindle Edition.

of you in the name of Jesus Christ for the forgiveness of your sins, and you will receive the gift of the Holy Spirit'" (Acts 2:38). As I mentioned in earlier chapters, the apostles sometimes included baptism in the call to conversion. But as I also mentioned, they were careful to distinguish that salvation was applied through faith, not baptism (cf. Acts 15:8-10). The epistles affirm that same fundamental truth (cf. Rom. 3:28; Eph. 2:8-10; Gal. 2:16). On the Day of Pentecost, receiving baptism would mark a public break with Judaism and require that person to solely identify with the Lord Jesus Christ having trusted in his person and work for salvation. In the truest sense, it would require those Jews listening to Peter's message to forsake everything in order to follow Christ (cf. Luke 14:33). The Holy Spirit, who inspired Peter's message, obviously made no provision that day for undisclosed conversions. For all "those who received his word were baptized, and there were added that day about three thousand souls" (Acts 2:41). If we allow Acts 2:38 to stand alone with those few passages that may appear to support baptismal salvation, then we will pervert the clear doctrine of salvation. However, if we understand what was at stake for those Jews listening to Peter's message at Pentecost, we can easily see why baptism was included in the call to conversion.

Acts 22:16

In Acts 22, Paul is speaking to a mob in Jerusalem. He is recalling his conversion experience that occurred on the Road to Damascus. After being blinded on his journey, he was told by the risen Christ to go into Demascus and wait for further instruction. Upon entering the town he was met by Ananias, a fellow believer, who said, "Brother Saul, receive your sight" (Acts 22:13). He then adds, "Rise and be baptized and wash away your sins, calling on his name" (Acts 22:16).

In must be noted that Acts records three separate accounts of Paul's conversion (cf. Acts 9:1-19, 22:1-21, 26:12-23). As mentioned in earlier chapters, the normal order of salvation is as follows:

a) *a person hears the gospel*
b) *a person repents and believes in Christ*
c) *a person is indwelt and filled with the Holy Spirit*
d) *a person receives water baptism as a public profession of faith*

Furthermore, any person indwelt and subsequently filled by the Holy Spirit is spiritually saved (cf. Rom. 8:9; 1 Cor. 12:13; Eph. 1:13-14). When these accounts are evaluated closely, it is apparent Paul was indwelt and filled by the Holy Spirit before his baptism (cf. Acts 9:17-19). Although Paul's conversion experience does not fit the norm, his experience with Ananias was very similar to the experience recorded in Acts 8:14-16.

In the third account of Paul's conversion, Paul recounts the words of Christ. Jesus said, "But rise and stand upon your feet, for I have appeared to you for this purpose, to appoint you as a servant and witness to the things in which you have seen me and to those in which I will appear to you, delivering you from your people and from the Gentiles—to whom I am sending you to open their eyes, so that they may turn from darkness to light and from the power of Satan to God, that they may *receive forgiveness of sins and a place among those who are sanctified by faith in me"* (Acts 26:16-18, *emphasis added*). The emphasis is placed on faith, not baptism.

The washing away of one's sins (figuratively speaking) occurs in the moment of regeneration which is inseparable from initial faith (cf. Titus 3:5). However, this spiritual cleansing is obviously signified in water baptism (cf. Acts 22:16).

Romans 6:3-4

Romans 6:3-4 reads, "Do you not know that all of us who have been baptized into Christ Jesus were baptized into his death? We were buried therefore with him by baptism into death, in order that, just as Christ was raised from the dead by the glory of the Father, we too might walk in newness of life." This passage comes in response to the question, "How can we who died to sin still live in it?" (Rom. 6:2). There are two ways to approach this passage. We can suggest that our union with Christ's death and resurrection occur during the act of baptism, or we can suggest that baptism signifies the spiritual reality that occurs in the moment a person believes. If we accept the former interpretation, Paul's arguments running from Romans 3:21 - 5:5 that center on the concept of justification by faith are rather pointless. In fact, to accept this interpretation makes the comparison between Abraham and the New Testament believer null and void. The latter interpretation, however, appears to be most fitting for several reasons. For starters, most commentators have argued that Paul begins his teaching on sanctification in Romans 6:1. How appropriate for Paul to reference baptism at the outset of this section knowing that baptism is or should be our first act of obedience as Christians. Secondly, this section of Scripture contains strong figurative overtones. For example, Paul states, "For if we have been joined with Him in the *likeness* of His death, we will certainly also be in the *likeness* of his resurrection" (Rom. 6:5, *emphasis added*). The use of that language suggests Paul is describing what baptism signifies, not the actual results of baptism (cf. Acts 22:16). When a person becomes a Christian he or she is brought into an intimate union with Jesus Christ. That person is said to have died with Christ and risen to new life (cf. Gal. 2:20). Water baptism signifies that spiritual reality, but does not produce it.

Colossians 2:11-12

"In him also you were circumcised with a circumcision made without hands, by putting off the body of the flesh, by the circumcision of Christ, having been buried with him in baptism, in which you were also raised with him through faith in the powerful working of God, who raised him from the dead" (Col. 2:11-12). Throughout his letter to the Colossians, Paul is exposing error and countering the fallacies of the false religions in Colossae. In the immediate context, Paul warns, "See to it that no one takes you captive by philosophy and empty deceit, according to human tradition, according to the elemental spirits of the world, and not according to Christ" (Col. 2:8). The comments that follow are reasons why Christ is fully sufficient for the believer. As Paul explains, in Christ "the whole fullness of deity dwells bodily" (Col. 2:9). In addition, the Colossians had "been filled in him, who is the head of all rule and authority" (Col. 2:10). Paul's use of *peplērōmenoi* (filled or complete) is in the perfect tense which illustrates this past action of being filled in Christ has enduring results. Colossians 2:11-12 explains at which point this filling occurred in the lives of his readers.

First, Paul explains, "In him you were circumcised with a circumcision made without hands," (Col. 2:11). Paul's opposition insisted on adhering to rituals or rites to secure final acceptance with God. Consequently, Paul counters by informing the Colossians they had also experienced a rite that made them fully acceptable to God. The rite he is referring to is circumcision. However, Paul is not referring to physical circumcision, but to a spiritual circumcision. As he points out, this was a circumcision "made without hands" (Col. 2:11). Notably, the use of *acheiropoiētos* occurs only three times in Scripture, each of which refers to an act performed not by *human* hands, but by God (cf. Mark 14:48; 2 Cor. 5:1). Evidently Paul is using circumcision as a metaphor referring to an inward change of the heart. This figurative use of circumcision is consistent throughout both the Old and New Testament (cf. Jer. 9:25-26; Deut. 10:14-16, 30:5-6; Rom. 2:29). It best describes the radical effects that occur upon the soul during the act of regeneration.

Secondly, Paul explains the effect of this circumcision;

"by putting off the body of the flesh, by the circumcision of Christ" (Col. 2:11). Although alternative interpretations exist for περιτομῇ τοῦ χριστοῦ, it seems most fitting that Paul is describing a spiritual surgery that Christ performs on all believers. During this surgery, Christ removes the dominating power of our inherent sin nature. In other words, the removal of "the body of the flesh" was a radical and spiritual act affected by the "circumcision made without hands" (Col. 2:11). Paul then adds, "having been buried with him in baptism, in which you were also raised with him through faith in the powerful working of God, who raised him from the dead" (Col. 2:12). Paul's argument presents a cause and effect relationship. This spiritual circumcision that was performed by Christ somehow plays a role in the believer's union with Christ in his death and resurrection. The burial mentioned in verse 12 is subsequent to the implied death in verse 11 referred to as "putting off the body of the flesh" (Col. 2:11).

But what does Paul mean by "burial with Him in baptism?" (Col. 2:12). Many contend that this reference is to water baptism. However, we have seen that the "circumcision made without hands" is the causal prerequisite to burial with Christ in baptism (Col. 2:11). One question must be raised. Since the circumcision the Colossians underwent was without hands, was the burial and rising in baptism not also without hands? As mentioned earlier, circumcision is neither "outward nor physical" (Rom. 2:28)? If Paul is referring to the act of regeneration, should we not expect that act to be a secret, unobservable act of God? As Christ explained, "The wind blows where it wishes, and you hear its sound, but you do not know where it comes from or where it goes. So it is with everyone who is born of the Spirit" (John 3:8).

So, is water baptism truly in view or that which water baptism signifies – union with Christ in His burial and resurrection? From our discussion thus far, it seems evident that it must be the latter. Paul is not teaching that burial with Christ in water baptism was immediately preceded by their "circumcision made without hands" (Col. 2:11). How could Paul enforce that claim (cf. 1 Cor. 1:16)? How could he know that they were baptized in water immediately upon their regeneration? He could not. However, he would understand that all who were circumcised of heart were inseparably buried and raised with Christ in spiritual baptism affected through faith (cf. 1 Cor. 12:13; Gal. 2:16, 20-21).

This interpretation finds further support as Paul explains "in which you were also raised with him through faith" (Col. 2:12). The prepositional phrase "through faith" indicates the means by which the Colossians were raised in baptism with Christ. This is the first mentioning of a human response in the text, and it must initiate as a result of being circumcised "without hands." In other words, those who experience the circumcision "made without hands" inseparably experience these other spiritual events, being both buried and raised with Christ through faith. This relationship between regeneration and the exercising of faith has long been upheld by Reformed Theologians.

There is another reason why Paul cannot be referring to water baptism in this text. For many who are water baptized do not possess genuine faith (cf. Acts 8:14-24).

The ones described here, however, have exercised faith as a means or instrument through which they were united to Christ in His burial and resurrection. A supporting example can be found in Acts. As Luke records, "To him all the prophets bear witness that everyone who believes in him receives forgiveness of sins through his name. While Peter was still saying these things, the Holy Spirit fell on all who heard the word" (Acts 10:43-44). As John MacArthur observes, "While Peter was still speaking these words his sermon was suddenly and dramatically interrupted. Without the text saying so, it is apparent that when Cornelius and the other Gentiles heard that forgiveness was available through Jesus Christ, they believed. In immediate response to their faith, the Holy Spirit fell upon all those who were listening to the message.[85]" Notably, when Peter was recalling this event to those in Jerusalem, he explained that he was told to deliver a message by which the Gentiles would be saved. He continued, "As I began to speak, the Holy Spirit fell on them just as on us at the beginning" (Acts 11:15) [86]. Peter

---

[85] MacArthur, John. *Acts 1-12: The MacArthur New Testament Commentary (Macarthur New Testament Commentary Series)* Chicago: Moody Publishers, 1991. (p. 295). Nook Edition.

[86] Some commentators would like to see a discrepancy between Peter's comment "As I began to speak" in Acts 11:15 and "while Peter was still saying these things" in Acts 10:44. According to the account recorded in Acts 10, the Spirit's indwelling presence was revealed at the end of Peter's invitation to exercise faith in Christ. One cannot forget the context of this setting; Peter probably doubted to some extent the notion that Gentiles, who were always considered unclean in the mind of the Jew, would embrace Christ. To assume that Luke's account recorded in Acts 10 is an

reached the climax of his narration, telling how he had scarcely begun to address Cornelius and his household when the Holy Spirit descended on them, just as he had descended on Peter and his fellow-disciples at Pentecost.[87] He then said, "And I remembered the word of the Lord, how he said, 'John baptized with water, but you will be baptized with the Holy Spirit.' If then God gave the same gift to them as he gave to us when *we believed in the Lord Jesus Christ*, who was I that I could stand in God's way"? (Acts 11:16-17; *emphasis added*). Peter indicates, like Paul, that spiritual baptism is predicated on believing in Jesus Christ (1 Cor. 12:13; Col. 2:11-12). Unity with Christ through reception of the Spirit is implied.

To summarize Paul's argument, Christians are complete in Christ because they have received a circumcision made without hands – regeneration. Regeneration produces faith that vitally unites souls to Christ. This vital union with Christ is a spiritual baptism that results in a complex of spiritual privileges, namely death and resurrection. If we want to use the word *baptizo*

---

interpolation rather than a chronological description seems to hold little value or support from Scripture. The account recorded in Acts 15.7-11 alone reaffirms that the Spirit was given when God saw the internal act of faith exercised by these Gentiles. All three of the accounts relating to this event recorded in Acts explain that baptism followed salvation and did not procure it (cf. Acts 10:47; Acts 11-17; Acts 15:7-11). When we look to the epistles for support of this claim, the evidence, in my opinion, is clear; the Spirit is received through faith, not works.

[87] Bruce, F.F. *The Book of Acts (New International Commentary on the New Testament)*. Grand Rapids: Wm. B. Eerdmans Publishing Co., 1988. (p. 222). Kindle Edition

(baptize) in its correct sense, we should be more inclined to use the word "immerse." Figurative uses of the word baptism can be found in 1 Corinthians 10:2 and 12:13 (see also 1 Corinthians 6:17, Galatians 3:27, and Ephesians 2:5). In the truest sense, baptism refers to the placing of a person, place, or thing into a new environment as to alter its condition or relationship to its previous environment. This is true of both spiritual and water baptism. When a person puts their trust in Christ, by some divine miracle that person is united with Christ in his death and resurrection. All of this may be typified by water baptism, though it is certainly not affected by it.

1 Peter 3:21

"Baptism, which corresponds to this, now saves you, not as a removal of dirt from the body but as an appeal to God for a good conscience, through the resurrection of Jesus Christ" (1 Pet. 3:21). This passage is also part of a larger context. In the days of Noah, God pronounced judgment on the earth (cf. Gen. 6:3). In spite of that, he allotted one hundred and twenty years for individuals to repent. As we know, only "eight persons were brought safely through water" (1 Peter 3:20). The antecedent to "this" in 1 Peter 3:21 refers to this preservation of Noah's family that occurred during the flood. The ark then served as a means of salvation during God's judgment on the wicked. Peter evidently sees a New Testament counterpart to this Old Testament historical event. According to Peter, the New Testament counterpart is baptism. Evidently baptism, whether spiritual or water, is salvific.

In the grand scheme of things, Peter is telling his readers that God preserves those who belong to Christ from his judgment or wrath just as He preserved Noah and his family from the earlier judgment on the earth. But why did Peter specifically say, "Baptism...saves you?" (1 Pet. 3:21). Although Peter was well aware of the baptism with the Holy Spirit, I don't believe he's referring to spiritual baptism in this passage (cf. Acts 10:44-48). In this instance, I believe Peter is referring to water baptism. Like I've mentioned before, our biblical authors connect baptism to our conversion experience. Peter, however, adds some additional language here that clarifies his statement. Baptism that simply removes dirt from the flesh is useless (Acts 8:13, 21). However, baptism that serves "an appeal to God for a good conscience, through the resurrection of Jesus Christ" has saving results. It appears in this instance Peter is connecting baptism with belief, even though initial faith and baptism are two separate actions that occur at different times. In other words, when a person receives baptism having appealed to God for a good conscience through faith in Christ, that baptism (here being described a shorthand for our conversion) is salvific. As always, a proper tension must be held between faith and baptism.

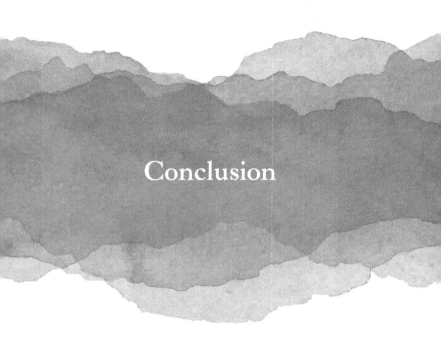

Conclusion

In conclusion, I hope this material will benefit someone looking to build or better their understanding on the subject of baptism. Sadly, this subject doesn't always receive the attention it deserves. From my experience, some churches teach that water baptism results in salvation. Still others downplay water baptism and all but remove it from their teaching or practice. Neither position does justice to our biblical text. I placed my trust in Christ years ago, and although I trust my justification occurred in the very moment I believed, I did not feel complete until I underwent my baptism. Although those feelings were somewhat subjective, I trust those feelings are commonplace among many Christians. Hopefully the pastors who teach our next generation of church members will elevate baptism to its proper status, all while protecting the essential doctrine of justification by faith. To this end I will say, "Amen."

Printed in the United States
By Bookmasters